Canadian Estate Planning Made Easy

Terrance Hamilton Hall

(c) Terrance Hamilton Hall 2017

FriesenPress

Suite 300 - 990 Fort St
Victoria, BC, Canada, V8V 3K2
www.friesenpress.com

ISBN
978-1-4602-4268-1 (Hardcover)
978-1-4602-4269-8 (Paperback)
978-1-4602-4270-4 (eBook)

1. Law, Estates & Trusts

Distributed to the trade by The Ingram Book Company

TABLE OF CONTENTS

**PART A
INTRODUCTION**

**PART B:
TOOLS OF ESTATE PLANNING**

PART C
ESTATE PLANNING GOALS
& TOOLS TO ACHIEVE THEM

The author's contact is:

Mr. Terry Hall
802-421 Dalhousie St.
Amherstburg ON N9V 3L2
T: 519-551-3871
E: obempire@gmail.com

ABOUT THE AUTHOR

The author has worked In both the legal and financial fields for many years and holds licences for insurance, investments, law, and is a member of the legal bars of Ontario (Law Society of Upper Canada) and Quebec (Barreau du Quebec).

His degrees are Bachelor of Commerce (Queen's), Bachelor of Laws (Windsor), Licence en Droit Civil (Ottawa), Master of Laws (Ottawa), and Master of Arts in Foreign Affairs (Johns Hopkins School of Advanced International Studies).

His awards are many, including the McLeod Scholarship (Queen's), Dickson Prize (Ottawa), Department of Justice of Canada fellowships, Donner Foundation fellowships, and the Queen's Diamond Jubilee medal among others.

As a lawyer, he has appeared before many federal hearings, the Federal and Supreme Courts of Canada, and the Parliament of Canada.

PREFACE

As we age, we look for the advice of others. I wrote this book to empower the public with extensive knowledge of estate planning to be used before seeking professional advice.

This book is unique in several ways because it:

1. combines the many tools used by lawyers and financial advisors,

2. provides in footnotes backup authorities, using free websites such as www.CanLII.org, and

3. refers to the two legal systems of Canada: the English Common Law in all provinces except Quebec, and the Civil Law system in Quebec based on the French Napoleonic Code.

Although as Shaw opined that youth is wasted on the young, we can resist our aging as Alfred, Lord Tennyson, expressed in Ulysses:

> "We are not now that strength which in old days
> moved earth and heaven,
> that which we are, we are
> One equal temper of heroic hearts,
> Made weak by time and fate, but strong in will
> To strive, to seek, to find, and not to yield."

I hope that my book is beneficial to you as you strive and seek to find at this stage of your life.

ABBREVIATIONS IN FOOTNOTES

GENERALLY

CRA   Canada Revenue Agency

Provinces & Territories
   AB for Alberta
   BC for British Columbia
   MB for Manitoba
   NB for New Brunswick
   NL for Newfoundland & Labrador
   NT for Northwest Territories
   NS for Nova Scotia
   NU for Nunavut
   ON for Ontario
   PE for Prince Edward Island
   QC for Quebec
   SK for Saskatchewan
   YT for Yukon

LAWS

CCQ   Civil Code of Quebec, SQ 1991, c 4.
CCSM   Continuing Consolidation of Statutes of Manitoba
IA   Insurance Act of Ontario, RSO 1990, c I.8
IC   Canada Revenue Information Circular
IT   Canada Revenue Interpretation Bulletin
ITA   Income Tax Act, RSC 1985, c 1 (5th Supp.)
ITF   Canada Revenue Income Tax Folio
PBSA   Pension Benefits Standards Act, RSC 1985 c 32(2nd Supp)
PBSR   Pension Benefits Standards Regulations, 1985, SOR/87-19.

RS	Revised Statutes (eg. RSC for Revised Statutes of Canada)
S	statute (eg. SC for Statutes of Canada)
SLRA	Ontario Succession Law Reform Act, RSO 1990, c S.26
SOR	Statutory Orders and Regulations of Canada

COURTS OF LAW

CA	Court of Appeal (eg. SKCA for Saskatchewan Court of Appeal)
FCA	Federal Court of Appeal
FCTD	Federal Court Trial Division
HL	House of Lords (UK)
OCGD	Ontario Court General Division
PC	Privy Council of the House of Lords (UK)
QB	Queen's Bench (eg. SKQB for Saskatchewan Queen's Bench)
SC	Supreme/Superior Court (eg. QSC for Quebec Superior Court)
SCC	Supreme Court of Canada
TD	Trial Division
TAB	Tax Appeal Board
TCC	Tax Court of Canada
TRB	Tax Review Board

LAW REPORTS OF COURT CASES

(2^d)(3^d)	means a subsequent series of the reports
AC	Appeal Cases of House of Lords or Privy Council
ACWS	All Canada Weekly Summaries
AllER	All England Reports (UK)
CanLII	Canadian Legal Information Institute
Ch	Chancery Reports (UK)
DTC	Dominion Tax Cases
DLR	Dominion Law Reports
ER	English Reports
ETR	Estates & Trusts Reports
LRQB	Law Reports of Queen's Bench (UK)

OJ   Ontario Judgments
OLR   Ontario Law Reports
QBD   Queen's Bench Division (UK)
SCR   Supreme Court of Canada Reports
WWR   Western Weekly Reports

PART A

INTRODUCTION

CHAPTER 1

ESTATE PLANNING

1.1   What is estate planning?

1.2   What is your estate?

1.3   Why is it important?

1.4   What is involved?

1.5   Where will it be located?

1.1   WHAT IS ESTATE PLANNING?

The idea of estate planning is not difficult: manage your property during your lifetime, set out your wishes for after your death, and arrange for those wishes to be carried out.

1.2   WHAT IS YOUR ESTATE?

An estate, called "succession" in Quebec, consists of assets and liabilities.

Typical estate assets are:

- personal property (Quebec: "movables"[1]):

  bank accounts

  life insurance

  pensions (private, government)

---

[1]   CCQ arts 899-905.

registered products (eg. RRSP, RRIF)

life insurance products (insurance, annuity, funds)

investments (bonds, stocks, funds)

car, boat, art, household items

digital accounts: email, blog, Paypal, Facebook

- real property (Quebec:"immovables"):

family home

vacation property

business.

Liabilities are sometimes called "The Big Four":

- funeral expenses,

- debts, loans, mortgage, credit card balances,

- estate expenses, executor's compensation, and

- taxes and fees (probate tax & fee, income tax).

If you think that your estate will have difficulty paying the liabilities, then arrange for liquidity by making your bank account joint with a trusted person who will settle your affairs (chapter 6) or simply by naming your estate as beneficiary in registered plans or life insurance products (chapters 7-8).

1.3 WHY IS IT IMPORTANT?

Estate planning is important to protect against events and risks. We are living longer and health becomes a risk of early incapacity, disability, unforeseen expenses, or death. Living longer also means that you might outlive your money.

The markets are a risk because returns on the traditional retirement safe-havens, bonds and GICs, have been low. At other times, inflation has eaten up savings, and pensions do have shortfalls.

Government is always present with income tax, probate fees or taxes, foreign taxes, and those nasty government clawbacks of benefits for which you paid.

1.4 WHAT IS INVOLVED?
Five common sense steps:

Step 1:   Inventory: Inventory your estate.[see Appendix A]

Step 2:   Goals: Set goals for the estate, such as:

- to create liquidity,

- to protect your estate,

- to provide for people.

Step 3:   Reality: Assess step 2 in view of step 1.

Step 4:   Action: Plan using various tools.

Step 5:   Review: Review periodically steps 1-4.

1.5 WHERE WILL YOUR ESTATE BE LOCATED?
The residence of your estate depends on the location of its central management and control, for which an important factor is the majority of executors or trustees and not the beneficiaries.[2]

---

[2]   ITF-S6-F1-C1; *Fundy Settlement v Canada,* 2012 CanLII 14 (SCC).

CHAPTER 2
BEFORE YOU START

2.1 You need mental capacity

2.2 Will: Do you need one? Yes & No

2.3 Beneficiaries: common types

2.4 Taxes: some introductory notes

2.1 YOU NEED MENTAL CAPACITY

Before starting the planning process, you must have sufficient mental capacity to know what you are doing. Without capacity, the whole effort may be useless and invite costly challenges from your family. For mental capacity, you should be

- acting freely and voluntarily,

- understanding the nature and effect of your actions, and

- knowing the nature and extent of your property, who is to benefit or not from your estate, and your obligations to dependants.[3]

You may question your capacity if some of the following apply to you:

- a history of psychiatric problems,

- very advanced age,

---

[3] *Banks v. Goodfellow,* (1870) LR 5 QB 549;
Hall v. Bennett Estate, 2003 CanLII 7157 (OCA).

- sick or weak in hospital or heavily medicated,

- big change of instructions from your last planning, or

- exclusion of usual beneficiaries, such as family, in favour of unusual beneficiaries, such as your nurse or paid caregiver.

If you anticipate incapacity at some time in the future, (eg. it runs in the family), it is a good idea to make a will and powers of attorney (chapters 3, 4) while you are still capable.

Marriage of an incapable person can upset estate planning because the level of capacity to marry is low in comparison to capacity to make a will and powers of attorney. Such a marriage might be set aside as unconscionable, lacking independent legal advice, or fraudulent.[4]

2.2   WILL: DO YOU NEED ONE? YES & NO

Yes, you need a will if you have real estate, assets to be left to specific beneficiaries, or if you anticipate your own incapacity to deal with property later.

No, if you are simply leaving an asset (often money), sometimes in a contract in which you can designate beneficiaries. These are called "will-substitutes" in which an asset passes directly to the beneficiaries and outside your estate. The common will-substitutes, in order of ease of creation, are:

- Gifting (chapter 5),

- Joint Ownership (chapter 6),

- Registered Plans (chapter 7),

- Life Insurance Company Products (chapter 8), and

- Trusts (chapters 9 & 10).

---

[4]   *Banton v Banton*, 1998 CanLII 14926 (OCGD).
   Juzumas v Baron, 2012 CanLII 7220 (ONSC).

But if you die with assets and no will and no beneficiary designations, then an "intestacy" arises for which the provincial governments have laws for the disposition of your estate with possible unintended consequences.[5] Ensure that you have dealt with all of your assets, because forgotten assets may be subject to a partial intestacy.

2.3 BENEFICIARIES: COMMON TYPES

A beneficiary is someone who is given a benefit. The common types encountered in wills and contracts (eg. RRSP, life insurance) are:

- **"children"**

The term "children" can include those born in or out of wedlock, adopted, stepchildren, children born before or after a designation as a beneficiary.[6]

- **"primary" and "contingent or secondary"**

A primary beneficiary receives a distribution of property first but, if unavailable, then a contingent or secondary beneficiary steps up to receive the distribution of property. In Quebec, a contingent beneficiary is known as a "subrogated beneficiary."

- **"revocable and irrevocable"**

---

[5] eg. the SLRA has the following distributions:
No spouse--> all to children equally

- no spouse or children-->all to parents, other relatives

- no heirs--> all to province

- spouse only-->all to spouse

- spouse + children-->$200,000 to spouse + share balance.

[6] eg. Ontario *Children's Law Reform Act*, RSO 1990,c C.12, s 1(1); *Brule v Brule*, [1979] 2 SCR 343.

If you intend to change a beneficiary in the future, you would designate that person as revocable rather than irrevocable because the latter requires the beneficiary's consent for the following:

- to change or revoke the designation,

- to assign or transfer ownership of the product,

- to change the amount of insurance coverage, and

- to remove funds from the product (eg. loan).[7]

The irrevocable designation is often used to protect against creditors. In Quebec, a spousal designation is automatically irrevocable unless changed to revocable. If incapacity is a possibility, obtain a copy of the power of attorney of an irrevocable beneficiary to ensure that consent can be obtained when needed in the future.

Be careful in naming a minor as an irrevocable beneficiary because the minor cannot provide consent until reaching the age of majority.

Be clear in who and how a beneficiary is named, although a recent court case permitted "rectification" of a designation that did not reflect your true intention.[8]

A court may change designations, even those made irrevocably[9], based on remedies in chapter 15 (Court-imposed support):

- dependants' support legislation permitting a variance of your will, the touching of assets inside or outside your estate, and the binding of your estate to support orders,

- unjust enrichment for which remedies, such as a trust, can be imposed on property, or

---

[7]   eg. IA s 191.

[8]   *Love v Love*, 2013 CanLII 31 (SKCA).

[9]   *Matthews v Matthews*, 2012 CanLII 933 (ONSC);
      Harrison (1996), 67 ACWS (3d) 1160 (OCGD).

- a moral claim derived from your expressed intentions by will or memorandum or conduct.[10]

2.4   TAXES: SOME INTRODUCTORY NOTES

Taxes form a large part of estate planning. Some concepts repeat throughout this book and, consequently, they will be discussed here to avoid repetition later.

Which taxes?

The taxes in estate planning are income tax (federal & provincial) and probate tax or fee (provincial). There is no separate capital gains tax, estate tax, or gift tax but there is an income tax on capital gains. Before the 1972 tax reforms, there were federally an estate tax and gift tax and provincially (ON, QC, BC) a succession duty (a type of estate tax).

For income tax purposes, an estate is considered a taxable entity.[11] There are two different types of estates, the ordinary and the Graduated Rate Estate (GRE). The first pays tax at a top rate and the second at a graduated rate for three years and then at the top rate.[12]

Probate tax or fee is a provincial tax on the whole of an estate. In 1998, Ontario probate fees were found to be unconstitutional as an indirect tax, which required their re-casting as the present Estate Administrative Tax ("EAT").[13]

---

[10]   Moral entitlement is relevant in AB, BC, and ON.

[11]   ITA s104(2).

[12]   ITA s 122(1); 2014 Budget, top rate 29%, to be 33%.for 2016.

[13]   *Estate Administration Tax Act*, SO 1998, c 34;
Re Eurig, 1998 CanLII 801 (SCC).

Rollovers

Income tax can be deferred, often by using a "rollover" that transfers the transferor's cost base to the transferee so that taxable capital gains are not realized until the transferee's disposition of the property or decease.

An election can be made not to use a rollover and instead to pay the tax based on fair market value of the asset,[14] especially if there are offsetting losses, exemptions, or unused tax credits.

Income-splitting

The purpose of income-splitting is to reduce a family's income tax by shifting income and capital gains from a person in a higher tax bracket to a person in a lower tax bracket.[15] In addition to lower taxes paid, the clawback of government benefits, such as Old Age Security, may be avoided.

Attribution Rules

The income tax attribution rules can undo estate planning, especially income-splitting. The rules apply to a transfer or loan for which income and capital gains will be attributed back from the transferee to the transferor. The transfer or loan can be done:

- directly,

- through a third party,

- by a direction to pay, or

- by a loan guarantee.[16]

---

[14]   ITA s 70(6.2); *Musselwhite Estate v MNR* (1985), 39 DTC 608 (TCC).

[15]   *ITA* ss 74.1-74.5, 75, 75.2; IT-369R, 369RSR S.R., 510, 511R.

[16]   *ITA* ss 74.1-75; 56(2), (4.1)-(4.3); 120.4; IT-369R, 369RSR S.R., 510, 511R.; *McClurg v Canada*, 1990 CanLII 28 (SCC).

The payor's intention should always be *bone fide* (eg. education, transportation) and not to avoid taxes, which attracts the anti-avoidance provision (below). The rules are not a problem if no income or capital gains are expected after the transfer.

Anti-avoidance provision

In the past, tax laws were considered an intrusion on a person's life and were given a strict interpretation by the courts. Tax avoidance was legal because a person was expected to arrange affairs to avoid the payment of taxes. On the other hand, tax evasion, a situation where taxes were obviously due, was and is a punishable offence. This was known as the "Westminster Principle" wherein Lord Tomplin of the British House of Lords stated:

> "Every man is entitled, if he can, to order his affairs so as that the tax attaching under the appropriate Acts is less than it otherwise would be. If he succeeds in ordering them so as to secure this result, then, however unappreciative the Commissioners of Inland Revenue or his fellow taxpayers may be of his ingenuity, he cannot be compelled to pay an increased tax."[17]

This echoed the Bible's admonition:

> "Then came also tax collectors to be baptized, and said unto him, Master, what shall we do? And he said unto them, Collect no more than you are authorized to do." Luke 3: 12-13

Times changed and so did the House of Lords which later enunciated the "Ramsay Principle" of unravelling a transaction to see if its design involved bona fide purposes or artificial steps to avoid taxation, in which case taxes would be due.[18] Subsequently, tax authorities came to regard tax avoidance as contrary to law.

---

[17] *IRC v Duke of Westminster*, [1936] AC 1 (HL).

[18] *Ramsay v IRC*, [1982] AC 300 (HL).

The CRA has a provision called GAAR (General Anti-Avoidance Rule) that is aimed at "avoidance transactions." GAAR can upset estate plans and undo attempts to avoid income tax. An "avoidance transaction" has a purpose of avoiding taxation rather than a *bona fide* purpose outside of taxation, such as protection from creditors.[19]

On June 26, 2013, new legislation was enacted requiring the disclosure to the CRA of "reportable transactions" undertaken to avoid the payment of taxes and based upon advice for which a fee was paid.[20]

Canada is not alone in having GAAR, as European countries have similar provisions, such as the UK, France, Germany, Italy, Netherlands, and Spain. The driving force is national governments coping with the ability of wealthy individuals and multinational corporations to shift income around the world to avoid taxation.

Tax evasion will also be prevented by Canada joining over 100+ countries in the international agreement, Common Reporting Standards (CRS), with 80,000+ financial institutions obligated to provide to the CRA financial information on taxpayer accounts around the world.

[19]   ITA s 245; *The Queen v Canada Trustco Mortgage Corp.*, [2005] 2 SCR 601;
Lipson v R, 2009 CanLII 1 (SCC);
McLarty Family Trust v The Queen (2012), 66 DTC 1123 (p. 3122) (TCC).

[20]   *ITA* s 237.3.

PART B

TOOLS OF ESTATE PLANNING

INTRODUCTION TO TOOLS

Estate planning involves the use of a variety of tools to help you reach your estate planning goals. The next 8 chapters will equip you with the tools used by lawyers and financial advisors. They are set out here because they repeat with each goal in Part C "Estate Planning Goals and Tools to Achieve Them." The tools that you will meet are:

Chapter 3: Wills

Chapter 4: Powers of attorney

Chapter 5: Gifting

Chapter 6: Joint ownership

Chapter 7: Registered plans

Chapter 8: Products of life insurance companies

Chapter 9: Trusts: the basics

Chapter 10: Trusts: the types.

Once you have these tools, then you can explore your estate planning goals equipped with the same knowledge used by professionals in the field. You can either carry out your goals by yourself or instruct a professional to do so on your behalf.

CHAPTER 3

TOOLS

WILLS

3.1 What is a will?

3.2 Types of wills (alphabetically)

3.3 Types of gifts

3.4 Beneficiaries

3.5 Correcting a mistake

3.6 Common problems with wills

3.7 What revokes a will?

3.8 What is probate and do you need it?

3.1 WHAT IS A WILL?

A will is a document outlining the distribution of your estate after death. When you make a will, you are called in law a "testator" from the French word for a will "testament." The person who you appoint in your will to do the distribution is called:

- an "executor," (pronounced "egg-zek-u-tor") in most cases,

- in Ontario an "estate trustee," and

- in Quebec a "liquidator."

The person receiving estate property is a beneficiary.

The French words entered the English language when French became the official language of England for several hundred years after the Norman conquest in 1066. To make a will understandable to both urban and rural people, a will used dual verbs as in the common expression "I devise and bequeath", with "devise" coming from the French verb "deviser" for the ruling urban class and "bequeath" from Old English for the rural Anglo-Saxon class, both words meaning "to give."

Remember to update your will if there are important life changes, such as marriage, death of your executor or of a beneficiary, and generally, you should review it every 5 years. Surprisingly, 65% of Canadians do not have a will.[21]

3.2 TYPES OF WILLS (alphabetically)

Attested Will (The Standard)
A will signed by the testator and then by witnesses, all in each other's presence at the same time.[22] The witnesses cannot be minors nor beneficiaries or their spouses.

---

[21] LawPro Magazine (Toronto: Lawyers' Professional Indemnity Co, 9/2015) vol 14.3 at 2.

[22] *Wills Act* in the provinces of MB, NB, NL, NS, NT, SK, YT-->
  CCSM, c W150; RSNB 1973, c W-9;
  RSNL 1990, c W-10; RSNS 1989, c 505; RSNWT 1988, c W-5.
  SS 1996, c W-14.1; RSY 2002, c 230.
AB: *Wills and Succession Act*, SA 2010, c W-12.2;
BC.: *Wills, Estates and Successions Act*, SBC 2009, c 13;
ON: *Succession Law Reform Act*, RSO 1990, c S.26;
PE: *Probate Act*, RSPEI 1988, c P-21;
QC: *Civil Code of Quebec*, arts 712-730.

Foreign Will

A will made in a foreign jurisdiction and recognized by provincial legislation if the will complies with the law of the place where it was made, or where the testator had domicile or habitual residence.[23]

Holograph Will

A will handwritten and signed by the testator.[24] An example was the farmer trapped under his overturned tractor who scratched his holograph will on the fender, which was brought into court.

International Will

A will used for assets in more than one international jurisdiction and, although provincial wills legislation recognizes it, few countries unfortunately subscribe to its supporting international convention.[25]

Joint Wills

An older type of will, sometimes in Civil Law jurisdictions, that is a single document containing the wills of two or more people, often disposing of jointly owned property. To avoid interpretation difficulties, mirror wills are used today.

Memorandum

A memorandum is an unattested document. A "precatory" memorandum is merely a non-binding expression of wishes, whereas a "non-precatory" or legal memorandum is binding on the executor if it exists when the will is executed and to which express reference is made in the will.

---

[23] eg. *SLRA* s 37.

[24] eg. *SLRA* s 6; *CCQ* art 714; not recognized in BC and PE.

[25] eg. *SLRA* s 42: *Convention Providing a Uniform Law on the Form of an International Will.*

Mirror or Similar Wills

Separate, identical wills drafted usually for spouse/partners wherein each is beneficiary of the other's will but there is no implied agreement not to change the will, as in the case of mutual wills. To prevent a doubling of gifts to beneficiaries in the event of simultaneous deaths, a "survivorship clause" should be inserted so that one spouse must survive the other for 30 days before being entitled to the estate.[26]

Multiple Wills

Property is split into "primary" and "secondary" wills with the primary will dealing with assets subject to probate and the secondary covering all other assets.[27] Each will must contain a non-revocation clause for the other wills; otherwise, a later one revokes an earlier. A good idea is to list in one will the assets to which it applies and then in each other state that it applies to all assets except those in the other will. Be clear on which one pays estate debts. Provincial law usually permits probate on part of an estate.[28]

Mutual Wills

Mirror wills that have an implied agreement not to revoke the will after the other person dies or loses mental capacity.[29] Changes can be prevented either by a written agreement not to change or by an express trust regarding assets in each will. There should be a

---

[26] *Hall v McLaughlin Estate*, 2006 CanLII 23932 (OSC).

[27] *Granovsky Estate v Ontario*, 1998 CanLII 14913 (OCGD);
Re Kerzner Estate, 2008 CanLII 42020 (OSC);
Re Kaptyn Estate, 2008 CanLII 53123 (OSCJ)..

[28] eg. Ontario *Estates Act*, RSO 1990, c E.21, s 32(3).

[29] *Hall v McLaughlin Estate*, 2006 CanLII 23932 (OSC);
Edell v Sitzer, 2004 CanLII 654 (OCA);
Trotman v Thompson   2006 CanLII 4953 (OSC)
Brynelsen Estate v Verdeck, 2002 CanLII 187 (BCCA).

non-revocation clause in each will, enforceable by the imposition of a constructive trust (discussed in ch. 10). Revocation can occur during the parties' lifetimes, while both still have mental capacity, to be done usually by joint consent or marriage, or possibly by a unilateral revocation with notice to the other.

Notarial Will

A Quebec will made before a notary in the presence of one or more witnesses and signed by the notary, testator, and witnesses, in each other's presence at the same time.[30]

Privileged Will

A will of a sailor at sea or member of the armed forces that is written without witnesses but certified by an officer.[31]

Reciprocal Wills

Mirror wills including gifts made one in consideration of the other as in an enforceable contract. Unlike mutual wills, reciprocal wills do not have to cover the whole estate.

Stationery Will

A will created by a store-bought kit. Estate litigators enjoy challenging such wills because mistakes are often made, such as spouses wrongly signing each other's will, which the author has seen.

3.3   TYPES OF GIFTS

A gift in your will is sometimes called a "legacy" or "bequest."

---

[30]   *CCQ* arts 712-730.

[31]   eg. *SLRA* s 5.

Specific bequest

A specified object (eg. piano, auto), dollar amount, or percentage of an estate.

Residual Bequest

All or a percentage of the remainder of an estate after all specific bequests have been fulfilled.

Contingent Bequest

All or a share of an estate after some event, such as the prior death of a primary beneficiary.

Trust Remainder Bequest

Estate income is paid to a named beneficiary of a trust after whose death the remainder of capital passes to another, such as a charity.

3.4 BENEFICIARIES

In addition to the common types of beneficiaries mentioned in chapter 2, you may also encounter the following beneficiaries, designated as **"per capita", "per stirpes", and "issue."**

"Per Capita" means per head and usually refers to one generation. "Per Stirpes" means by representation. "Issue" means several generations and is used with "per stirpes." For example, if a testator had 2 children and each had 2 children, a per capita distribution would have 6 shares whereas a per stirpes distribution would have 2 shares and if a child predeceased, there would still be 2 shares with the predeceased's share split between that person's 2 children.[32]

If you intend to name in your will a beneficiary of a contract (eg. RRSP, life insurance), then:

1. check the contract for an earlier designation,

---

[32]   *Dice v Dice Estate*, 2012 CanLII 468 (ONCA).

2. identify the contract clearly,

3. ensure there are words included such as "and these proceeds shall not form part of my estate", and

4. realize that the beneficiary cannot be named irrevocably (because a will Is revocable).

If the designation fails, then the proceeds may pass into instead of outside the estate thereby encountering probate.

3.5 CORRECTING A MISTAKE

Mistakes are fixed by rectification, variation, or alteration. Contingent interests affected by a change can be protected using life insurance.

Rectification changes a will to achieve what the testator intended as in the case of a clerical error, a misunderstanding of instructions, or a failure to carry out instructions but it cannot be an amendment.[33]

Variation changes a will to carry out what was or what should have been the testator's intention.[34] If you want to prevent a variation in the future by others, then try the following:

- gifting while still alive (chapter 5),

- joint ownership of assets with right of survivorship (chapter 6),

- passing assets outside the estate, such as by beneficiary designations in contracts (eg. RRSP, life insurance) (chapters 7, 8),

---

[33] *Jean Coutu Group v Canada*, 2016 SCC 55 (CanLII)

Canada v Fairmount Hotels, 2016 SCC 56 (CanLII)

Daradick v McKeand Estate, 2012 CanLII 5622 (ONSC);

Cunningham v Quadrus Charitable Foundation, 2012 CanLII 5836 (ONSC)

Archambault v Canada, [2013] 3 SCR 838.

[34] *Tataryn v Tataryn Estate*, 1994 CanLII 51 (SCC); *Cummings v Cummings Estate*, 2004 CanLII 9339 (OCA).

- creating a trust while still alive (chapters 9, 10), or

- writing down reasons in the will if an unusual omission or inclusion is intentional, such as excluding an obvious beneficiary.

Alteration is a change in the testator's intention and is usually accomplished by a "codicil" (pronounced "cod-i-sil") executed in the same manner as the will. If extensive, it is easier to make a new will.

3.6 COMMON PROBLEMS WITH WILLS

Lack of Testamentary Capacity
Be careful if you are having difficulty with reality.

"Suspicious Circumstances"
Such circumstances cast doubt whether you were acting freely and voluntarily and not under the undue influence of another, such as a paid caregiver.[35]

Choosing an executor; Non-resident executor
You should choose an odd number of executors to prevent deadlock on decisions. Also, don't create the following situations:

- your spouse/partner is beneficiary of the will and also of a spousal trust in the will allowing her to encroach upon and use up the estate's capital to the detriment of other beneficiaries,

- incompatible family members as executors, and

- a business associate who favours the business over your wishes for your estate.

---

[35] *Vout v Hay*, 1995 CanLII 105 (SCC)..

Make your executor aware of his personal liability in administering your estate. Liability insurance is available for executors, for which you can provide payment of the premium in your will.

Watch out if you appoint a non-resident executor. That's acceptable for non-resident property but don't let that person have a controlling vote because the rest of your estate may then be governed by the law of that non-resident's location with unintended consequences. Where important, insert a clause into documents:

1. relieving control from or discharging an executor who becomes non-resident and

2. naming a resident as contingent executor to take the non-resident's place.

"No Contest" Clause or Remarriage Clause
This type of clause attempts to disinherit a beneficiary who contests the will or the spouse who remarries, but it is generally of no effect.

3.7 WHAT REVOKES A WILL?
You revoke your will when you make another will,[36] or declare the will void, or you destroy it, or remarry (in most provinces).[37] For divorce, usually provincial legislation presumes that your spouse predeceased you in order to be disinherited from your will but it is best to rewrite your will. The question of the effect on a will of a dissolution of a civil partnership is now being examined by the provincial governments.

If you revoke your will, you've also revoked beneficiary designations in it.[38] Note that the mere invalidity of your will for failure to follow formal requirements does not necessarily revoke a beneficiary

---

[36] eg. *SLRA* ss15-17.

[37] But not necessarily in AB, BC, and QC.

[38] eg. *IA* ss 171, 192(3); *SLRA* s 52.

designation, which need only be signed without a witness. Revocation does not revive an earlier designation such that proceeds are paid into the estate.[39]

3.8 WHAT IS PROBATE AND DO I NEED IT?

Probate is a court process in the Common Law provinces to confirm that an executor has authority to deal with your estate and that your will is compliant with formality, is uncontested, and is the only one existing, all of which provides comfort to the public. In Quebec, the process is called "verification" but it is not required for a notarial will.

Probate is not always necessary. The executor's power to deal with your estate is based on the will itself and not on probate.

Probate was originally designed to finance the court structure when introduced during the reign of King Edward IV in the 15th century. The term "probate" derives from the Latin verb "probo, probare" meaning "to prove."

The court will issue probate documents to you in the form of Letters Probate if you have a will and Letters of Administration if you do not. In Ontario, the corresponding documents are Certificate of Appointment of Estate Trustee With a Will, or Without a Will.

The court process can follow either the "common form" with the mere filing of documents or "solemn form" with witnesses in court.

Probate can result In a provincial tax or fee, the avoidance of which is not always a worthwhile strategy depending on the province:

- highest probate tax: ON, BC, NS

- lower tax: MB, NB, NL, PE, SK

- lowest tax: AB, NT, YT

- no tax: QC.

---

[39] eg. *IA* s192; *SLRA* s 52; *Petch v Kuivila*, 2012 CanLII 6131 (ONSC).

Probate has problems. Firstly, probate tax or fees are regarded as non-deductible for income tax on your estate nor are they added to the cost base of properties, but possibly this is changing.[40] Secondly, delays in processing can deny access to funds to pay liabilities, gifts, support for dependants, and might interfere with the continuation of a business. Thirdly, probated documents are public so that you lose privacy and confidentiality. Lastly, probate cannot be avoided on some assets, such as real estate, unless an exemption applies.

An expression "double probate" arises when your beneficiary survives long enough to receive the assets and then dies, resulting in a second probate. This can be avoided by including in your will a "survivorship clause" requiring a beneficiary to survive you by say, 30 days, before being entitled to the estate.

Probate can be avoided by preventing property from entering into your estate, using multiple wills, gifting (chapter 5), joint ownership (chapter 6), naming beneficiaries in and successor owners of life insurance and registered products (chapters 7, 8), and trusts outside your will (chapters 9, 10).

---

[40]   *CRA Guide T4011;*
       Brosamler v The Queen, 2012 CanLII 204 (TCC).

CHAPTER 4

TOOLS

POWERS OF ATTORNEY

4.1 **What is a power of attorney?**

4.2 **Do you need a power of attorney?**

4.3 **Types of powers**

4.4 **How is a power created?**

4.5 **When is it effective and its duration?**

4.6 **Are there limits on an attorney?**

4.7 **Alternative to a power**

4.1 WHAT IS A POWER OF ATTORNEY?

A power is a document by which you ("grantor") give to another person ("attorney") power to act on your behalf. In Quebec, a power is called a "mandate," the grantor is a "mandator," an attorney is a "mandatary," and the law is similar to the Common Law provinces. In BC, an attorney is called a "representative."

4.2 DO YOU NEED A POWER OF ATTORNEY?

Yes, a power of attorney is handy if you will need someone in the future to act in your best interest when you cannot do so for yourself. Without a power of attorney, the provincial government will manage your affairs if you are incapacitated. Provincial legislation provides for powers of attorney.[41] The acronym for a power in legal and financial parlance is "P.O.A."

4.3 TYPES OF POWERS

A power can deal with property or health, be verbal or written, general or limited (eg. time, place, or duration) or specific as to scope.

4.4 HOW IS A POWER CREATED?

You must have mental capacity, for which the tests are less stringent than for a will, and involve an awareness of:

- for property:

  - the nature and value of your property and awareness that they may decline in value or be misused by the attorney, who must account for his activity,

  - your obligations to dependants, and

  - your ability to revoke the power;

- for personal care and health:

---

[41] AB: *Personal Directives Act*, RSA 2000, c.P-6;

BC: *Representation Agreement Act*, RSBC 1996, c. 405;

MB: *Health Care Directives Act*, CCSM c. H27;

NB: *Infirm Persons Act*, RSNB 1973, c. I-8;

NL: *Advance Health Care Directives Act*, SNL 1995, c. A-4.1;

NS: *Personal Directives Act*, SNS 2008, c.8;

NT: *Personal Directives Act*, SNWT 2005, c. 16;

ON: *Substitute Decisions Act*, SO 1992, c.30;

PE: *Consent To Treatment and Health Care Directives Act*, SPEI 1996, c. C-17.2;

QC: CCQ art. 2130-2185;

SK: *Health Care Directives and Substitute Health Care Decision Makers Act*, SS 1997, c. H-0.001;

YT: *Care Consent Act*, SY 2003, c. 21, sch B.

- the attorney's concern for your welfare when making decisions for you.[42]

Next, an attorney is chosen, usually your spouse/partner or relative. A paid caregiver is generally not an attorney. "Joint and several" attorneys are recommended to avoid the situation of death or incapacity of an attorney and also a deadlock in decision-making.

The formalities are a written document witnessed by two persons who cannot be the attorney, your spouse/partner, your child or a minor, nor the spouse/partner of the attorney.

4.5 WHEN IS IT EFFECTIVE AND ITS DURATION?

A power is effective once signed unless it is conditional on or limited to a specific time, care, or contingency, such as incapacity.

A limited power ends upon the expiry of its limitation. Generally, a power terminates upon your death, bankruptcy, or mental incapacity, which is the reason for legislation creating "continuing" or "enduring" powers to survive mental incapacity. A continuing power for personal care is sometimes referred to as a "health care proxy or directive, advance directive, or living will" although the living will is usually a mere expression of wishes for treatment without appointing someone to act on your behalf.

Revocation of a power is in the same manner in which it was created. Divorce does not revoke a power of attorney and, consequently, you must rewrite it.

4.6 ARE THERE LIMITS ON AN ATTORNEY?

You can place any limits but generally an attorney cannot:

- delegate authority nor perform an act requiring your personal knowledge, such as swearing an affidavit,

---

[42] Substitute Decisions Act, 1992, SO 1992, c 30 as am, ss 8, 47; *Egli v Egli*, 2004 CanLII 529 (BCSC), aff'd 2005 CanLII 627 (CA).

- make, change or revoke a will,[43] or

- personally benefit or have a conflict of interest unless the particular event is permitted by the power or by law, such as supporting a dependant.[44]

The courts have interpreted "make, change or revoke a will" quite broadly such that, in the absence of specific terms in the power or demonstrated benefit for you, an attorney cannot frustrate your will (nor family law legislation) through the sale, gifting or removal of assets, opening a joint account, altering a trust, nor dealing with the matrimonial home. Except in BC, an attorney cannot change beneficiaries in a contract (eg life insurance, registered products).[45]

Estate planning is permitted if you probably will not recover capacity, the plan will result in tax savings to you without capital dispositions, and sufficient assets are available to provide for your needs.[46]

4.7 ALTERNATIVE TO A POWER
An alternative to a power of attorney is a trust because:

- the standard of care of a trustee is more certain and higher,

- comprehensive trustee duties can be listed,

- a trustee's legal title comforts third parties and financial institutions,

---

[43]   *Desharnais v TD Bank,* 2002 CanLII 640 (BCCA).

[44]   *Re Goodman,* 1998 CanLII 3902 (BCSC).

[45]   *Richardson Estate v Mew,* (2009) CanLII 403 (CA);
BC Power of Attorney Act, s. 20(5).
Easingwood v Cockroft, 2013 CanLII 182 (BCCA);
Pecore v Pecore, 2007 CanLII 17 (SCC);
Madsen v Saylor, 2007 CanLII 18 (SCC).

[46]   *O'Hagan v O'Hagan,* 2000 CanLII 79 (BCCA).

- potential abuse of the owner is reduced by his removal from decision-making,

- a trustee can manage property out of the jurisdiction,

- instructions can be given for gifts and charitable bequests, and

- a trust survives death whereas a power does not.

Another alternative is a court-appointed guardian (Quebec "curator" or "tutor").

CHAPTER 5

TOOLS

GIFTING
(While you are alive)

Giving things away is called "gifting." When you gift, you are known as a "donor" and the recipient is the "donee." The law requires three elements to be present:

1. a donor's intention to give,

2. a donee's acceptance, and

3. an act of delivery without any particular formality required.

Mental capacity again plays a part. You must have capacity and freely intend to transfer property to the donee who must have capacity to accept the gift and so intends. A gift by a minor is voidable, meaning it may be valid or invalid, depending on the minor's intentions. If a gift is to be rejected, a disclaimer of the gift must be done before acceptance.[47]

Some activities are not gifts. A giving of property but expecting it back at some time is a loan and not a gift. If the donee was giving

---

[47] *Teixeira v Markgraf,* 2017 CanLII 427 ONSC. ITF-S6-F2-C1.

something back to you in return, that would not be a gift but a bargain.[48] To avoid a bargain or a loan, you must be clear in your intention and have done all necessary to transfer the property in a complete, effective, and irrevocable manner.

Income tax! Yes, gifting can be regarded as a disposition for income tax purposes but no tax will be due if the property is non-appreciating (cash or near-cash)[49] or appreciating with offsetting tax losses, credits, or exemptions. If gifting to your family, watch out for the attribution rules that can send income and possibly capital gains back to you.

There is no probate tax because you're still alive; so, the gift is considered to be living and not testamentary.[50]

If you want to gift an asset after death but retain control during your lifetime, then gift the remainder interest only and retain a life interest. The creation of the remainder interest is a taxable disposition. At your decease, the remainder person bears the tax of any capital gains arising from the time of the original gift.[51]

Deathbed gifts have a special latin name in law, "donatio mortis causa." This is a gift just before death or in contemplation of and conditional upon your death. The important point is that you give control of the property to the donee. Delivery of the property can

---

[48]   *Kooner v Kooner* 1979 CanLII 448 (BCSC);
        McNamee v McNamee, 2011 CanLII 533 (ONCA);
        Buttar v Buttar, 2013 CanLII 517 (ONCA);
        Cochrane v Moore (1890), 25 QBD 57 (CA).

[49]   *ITA* ss 69(1)(b); IT-209R & 209RSR.

[50]   *Brown v Rotenberg*, 1946 CanLII 101 (OCA).

[51]   *ITA* s 43.1.

be actual or constructive.[52] Land (real property) is not included.[53] In Quebec Civil Law, such a gift is "mortis causa" and is limited to your spouse and children (present & future).[54]

---

[52]   *Re Calaiezzi Estate,* [1993] OJ No 2863 (OCGD);
       Re Smith Estate, 1995 CanLII 10500 (NLTD).

[53]   *Dyck v Cardon* (1984), 17 ETR 54 (ABCA).

[54]   *CCQ* arts1840-1841.

CHAPTER 6

TOOLS

JOINT OWNERSHIP

When you own something with another person, then you have "joint ownership," which can be divided or undivided.

If divided, then you control your portion and the other person controls her portion. In Common Law, the divided type is called a "tenancy in common;" in Quebec Civil Law it is called "undivided co-ownership." At death, the deceased's portion passes to her estate and not to you, the survivor.

If you each can control the whole property, then that is undivided ownership. In Common Law, the undivided type is called a "joint tenancy." There is no equivalent in Quebec Civil Law. Usually a joint tenancy is combined with a "right of survivorship," (acronym: JTWROS) meaning that an owner's interest is extinguished at death and the survivor continues ownership and control of the whole. In joint ownership, the CRA presumes a joint tenancy with right of survivorship, unless proven to the contrary.

Be clear in your intention, such as:

- "A & B as joint owners with right of survivorship and not as tenants in common' or

- "A for 45% and B for 55% as tenants in common with no right of survivorship"

and in land transfers, such as:

- "jointly and not as tenants in common."[55]

If you are not clear, then a court will look at various factors to determine your intentions: documentation, actions and contributions, purpose of the account and its actual use.[56] Additionally, the surviving joint tenant may find himself holding the property not as owner but as trustee for others under a "resulting trust" (defined in chapter 10).

Joint tenancy with right of survivorship

Advantages

- Simplicity in transition of ownership at decease. Often only a death certificate is required in order to assume absolute ownership of the whole.

- Avoidance of the deceased's estate and probate.

- A recognition of ownership rights in the face of other claims, such as bankruptcy or dependant's relief, because there is no new transfer of property but an extinguishment of the deceased's rights.[57]

---

[55] eg. Ontario *Conveyancing and Law of Property Act*, RSO 1990, c C.34, s 13(1).

[56] *Pecore v Pecore,* 2007 CanLII 17 (SCC);
Madsen Estate v Saylor, 2007 CanLII 18 (SCC).

[57] *Madore-Ogilvie v Kulwartian,* 2006 CanLII 39034 (OSC Div);
Re Cameron Estate, 2011 CanLII 6471 (ONSC).

Disadvantages

- A potential re-classification as an "agency" and not joint ownership if your true intention was merely to have bills paid (often the parent-child situation)[58]

- The creation of joint ownership is a taxable disposition (except for spouses),[59] proportional to each contributor, which may trigger the attribution rules if one owner contributes all or most of the assets.

- Changes require the consent of both owners but if one becomes incapacitated, then change becomes complicated.

- Exposure to creditors of all owners.

- Risk of a joint owner severing a joint tenancy, thereby creating a tenancy in common that can be disposed separately unless there is an agreement to the contrary.[60]

- The joint interest cannot pass in a will because the right of survivorship takes precedence.[61]

- A surviving spouse might share in an estate more than expected if claiming both joint property outside the estate by a right of survivorship and also an equalization payment from the estate under family law legislation (discussed in chapter 12).

---

[58] *ITA* ss 69(1), 70(5); *Pecore v Pecore*, 2007 CanLII 17 (SCC); *Madsen Estate v Saylor*, 2007 CanLII 18 (SCC).

[59] *ITA* ss 69(1)(b), 70(5).

[60] *Robichaud v Watson*, 1983 CanLII 1701 (OSC); *Lam v Le Estate*, 2002 CanLII 31 (MBQB)..

[61] *Sorensen's Estate v Sorensen* (1979), 90 DLR(3d) 26 (ABCA), appeal to SCC discontinued [1979] 1 SCR xiii.

A solution to some of these problems is to have the owners sign contracts and make codicils to their wills that, upon death, the estate of the deceased will not claim an interest in the joint property.

The death of a joint owner is a taxable disposition of the deceased's portion of the property (usually 50%) payable by her estate and not by the survivor.

CHAPTER 7

TOOLS

REGISTERED PLANS
(alphabetically)

Registered plans are tax-efficient savings plans registered with the federal or provincial governments. You own the plan and are also its measuring life, called an "annuitant." You can name beneficiaries. A reference below to a "dependent (grand)child" means a child or grandchild who is dependent on you financially or owing to mental or physical infirmity.

Remember that if you intend to name in your will a beneficiary of a registered product, then:

1. identify the contract clearly, and

2. ensure there are words included such as "and these proceeds shall not form part of my estate;"

otherwise, the proceeds may pass into instead of outside the estate thereby attracting probate. A naming of a beneficiary in your will can override an earlier designation in a contract; so, when drafting a will, check whether a designation in a contract is being overridden.

In Quebec, a beneficiary of a product has to be named in your will or marriage contract, not in the product, unless purchased from a life insurance company.[62]

There are many plans, individual and group, but the following discussion will deal with individual plans important for estate planning.

DPSP

A Deferred Profit-Sharing Plan (DPSP) resembles a pension plan in which an employer makes contributions that are taxed only when received by the employee, usually in retirement. Contributions are made from current or accrued profits. A plan is useful to a smaller company unsure of profitability and unable to make regular contributions to a pension plan. A plan is not available to an owner or major shareholder of a company.

IPP

An Individual Pension Plan (IPP) is an employer-sponsored, defined-benefit Registered Pension Plan (RPP) for an individual or for a family working in a business. Typically, it is used by business owners, key executives, and self-employed professionals to maximize their retirement benefits.[63] The advantages are:

- guaranteed lifetime income in retirement,

- higher contribution rate than a RRSP, leading to a higher accumulation for retirement,

- contributions allow a past-service catch-up by transferring RRSPs and other pensions into the IPP,

- setup costs, maintenance, and contributions are tax-deductible to the corporation,

---

[62]   *CCQ* arts 1819-1820.

[63]   *ITA* s147.1, Regu. 8300.

- avoidance of payroll tax, and

- protection from creditors of yourself and the corporation.

The disadvantages are:

- your annual income should be $100,000+,

- the employer must be incorporated and you must receive employment income from it,[64]

- contributions are locked-in, and

- annual contributions are mandatory.

LIF

A Life Income Fund (LIF) is a "Locked-In Registered Retirement Income Fund (RRIF)." Monies are received from a pension plan, LIRA, or LRSP. A LIF has a legislated minimum and maximum withdrawal requirement and can continue for a lifetime, although in the province of Newfoundland & Labrador an annuity must be purchased by age 80.[65] You can name a beneficiary, and also name your spouse/partner as the successor annuitant to receive continued payments.

Ontario has created a "new" LIF to receive funds from an "old" LIF, pension plan, or LIRA. Old LIFs are no longer available for purchase but those existing can continue. An annuitant aged at least 55 can unlock up to 50% of the funds transferred to the new LIF. The unlocking occurs by a subsequent transfer to an unlocked RRSP or RRIF in the 60 days of the initial transfer. RRSP contribution room Is not affected and there is no withholding tax.

---

[64] *Jordan Financial v MNR*, 2007 CanLII 263 (FCA);
    1346687 Ontario Inc. v MNR, 2007 CanLII 262 (FCA).

[65] *ITA* ss146.3, 147.3(1), *PBSA* s 20.1, *PBSR* s 2.

LIRA

A Locked-in Retirement Account (LIRA) is a "Locked-In Registered Retirement Savings Plan (RRSP)" that receives pension monies when employment terminates.[66] A Registered Pension Plan (RPP) can be rolled into a LIRA that operates like a RRSP until age 71 when you must roll it into a LIF or purchase an annuity. The removal of funds before age 71 is allowed for financial hardship, small balances, non-residency, or shortened life expectancy.

LRIF

A Locked-in Retirement Income Fund (LRIF) is a "Locked-In RRIF" and is more flexible than a LIF with payments based on investment performance. It receives funds from a LIF, LIRA, or RPP held in Newfoundland & Labrador (ceased in AB, MB, ON) and can continue for life without a requirement to purchase an annuity at a certain age.

LRSP

A Locked-In Retirement Savings Plan (LRSP) is a LIRA in BC and federally.

LSVCC

A Labour-sponsored Venture Capital Corporation (LSVCC) invests in start-up ventures and provides an income tax credit up to $5,000 for purchase of its shares.

PPP

A Personal Pension Plan resembles an IPP but with more flexibility and built-in costs.

---

[66]   *ITA* ss146(1), 147.3(1); *PBSA*, s 20, *PBSR* s 2.

PRIF

A Prescribed Retirement Income Fund (PRIF) is in Manitoba and Saskatchewan to receive funds from a pension plan, LIRA, or LIF. Unlike a LIF but similar to a RRIF, it permits money to be withdrawn without a maximum. In Saskatchewan, a PRIF replaced the LIF.

PRPP

A Pooled Registered Pension Plan (PRPP)[67] is a voluntary, low cost, portable, defined-contribution RPP administered by a regulated financial institution and not by an employer. The PRPP works within the limits for a RPP and RRSP. Plans are federal or provincial. At decease, the plan would be included in estate income unless the spouse/partner or dependant (grand)child is named as beneficiary who can rollover proceeds to their RPP, RRSP, RDSP, or used to purchase an annuity.[68]

RCA

A Retirement Compensation Arrangement (RCA) is set up by an employer to contribute tax-deductible funds to a trust for taxable payments to an executive upon retirement or substantial change in employment. Contributions do not reduce the employee's RRSP room and are protected from the employer's insolvency.

RDSP

A Registered Disability Savings Plan (RDSP) encourages long-term savings to provide income for a disabled individual.[69] The plan's creator is called the "account holder" and the disabled person is the beneficiary, who must be a Canadian resident, less than 60 years old, and must qualify for the Disability Income Tax Credit. A disabled

---

[67]   *ITA s 147.5.*

[68]   ITA ss 147.5, 60(1), Tax Guide T4040.

[69]   *ITA s 146.4.*

person can be both account holder and beneficiary. There can be several holders but only one beneficiary and one plan. If the disabled person is a minor or lacks mental capacity, then a family member (parent, spouse/partner) or guardian can create the plan.

Contributions are not tax deductible and growth within the plan is tax-deferred. The lifetime contribution limit is $200,000 with no annual limit and contributions can be made to age 59. Up to age 49, federal contributions are available in the form of the Canada Disability Savings Grant (CDSG) and Canada Disability Savings Bond (CDSB). The maximum lifetime limit for the CDSG is $70,000 and $20,000 for the CDSB. Contributions are owned by the beneficiary. Funds from a RRSP, RRIF, or RPP can rollover to a RDSP.

Withdrawals from a RDSP are in two forms: periodic Lifetime Disability Assistance Payments (LDAP) and lump-sum Disability Assistance Payments (DAP). Payments have a non-taxable portion (contributions) and a taxable portion (growth, government grants and bonds, rollover amounts). The holder and beneficiary are jointly and severally liable for taxes.[70] Withdrawals generally do not impact provincial programs but repayment of grants and bonds may be required, making a RDSP less attractive for short-term expenses unless life-expectancy is short, in which case a Specified Disability Savings Plan (SDSP) may be set up for payments.

RESP

A Registered Education Savings Plan (RESP) encourages saving for post-secondary education through the tax-deferred growth of con-tributions.[71] A RESP is not a trust and is owned by a subscriber, not the beneficiary. The plan can be used not just for children but also for adults returning to school or for learning in retirement. The adult can be both subscriber and beneficiary.

---

[70]   *ITA* s 160.21.

[71]   *ITA* s 146.1.

The contributions are not tax-deductible, there is no annual limit, and they can total up to a lifetime limit of $50,000. The income tax attribution rules do not apply. Earnings accumulate tax-deferred in the plan. The plan must be wound up within 36 years.

If the beneficiary is less than age 18, then the RESP qualifies for the Canada Education Savings Grant (CESG), Canada Learning Bond (CLB), and provincial grants/credits in some provinces.[72] Above the age of 18, the grants are no longer available in which case the TFSA is probably a better tax-advantaged vehicle for education saving. If the beneficiary is disabled and unable to attend post-secondary education, then the investment income of a RESP can be transferred by rollover to a RDSP.

Once enrolled in an educational institution, a beneficiary is entitled to withdraw, without repayment of the grants:

- contributions as tax-free Post-Secondary Education Capital Redemptions (PSE), essentially as capital redemptions, and

- income and grants as taxable Educational Assistance Payments (EAPs).

If the beneficiary does not continue to post-secondary education, then the subscriber can withdraw contributions tax-free, government grants must be repaid, and if the plan has existed for 10 years, then earnings can be withdrawn as Accumulated Income Payments (AIPs) which can be:

- transferred to the subscriber's own RRSP or spousal RRSP (if sufficient room exists), or

- contributed at cost by rollover to the beneficiary's RDSP, or

- taken as income with a penalty tax of 20%.

---

[72]   AB, QC, SK.

RLIF

A Restricted Life Income Fund (RLIF) is federal, receives monies from a federal pension plan, LIF, LIRA or RLSP, has minimum and maximum withdrawal requirements, allows transfers to a RRSP or RRIF, can be held for life, and on a one-time basis unlocks 50% of its funds.[73]

RLSP

A Restricted Locked-In Savings Plan (RLSP), similar to a RRSP, allows a person aged less than 71 to return funds from a RLIF to a RLSP because retirement income is no longer needed.[74]

RPP

A Registered Pension Plan (RPP) comes in two varieties:

- a defined-benefit plan that guarantees a retirement payout amount, and

- a defined-contribution plan (or money-purchase plan) that has a set contribution but no guarantee on the payout.[75]

There has been a substantial shift in industry from the former plan to the latter where investment risk falls on the employee. Plans can be federal or provincial.[76]

---

[73] *ITA* s 146.3(1), *PBSA* s 20.3, *PBSR* s 2.

[74] *ITA* s 146(1), *PBSA*, s 20.2, *PBSR* s 2.

[75] *ITA* ss 147.1-147.3.

[76] *PBSA* in some provinces & federally:
　　　Federal, YT, NT--> use the federal act
　　　BC & ON--> RSBC 1996 c 352; RSO 1990, c P.8.
　　Pension Benefits Act in other provinces:
　　　MB, NB, NL, SK-->CCSM c P32; SNB 1987 c P-5.1;
　　　SNL 1996 c P-4.01; SS 1992 c P-6.001;
　　AB-->*Employment Pension Plans Act*, RSA 2000 c E-8;
　　QC--> *Supplemental Pension Plans Act*, RSQ c R-15.1.

Ontario has proposed in its 2014 budget to have a provincial RPP or ORPP to supplement the CPP for those without pensions.

The results at death vary but generally, a named beneficiary receives a lump sum payment (not periodic payments) which avoids probate but is taxable income to the beneficiary.[77] If no beneficiary is named, the proceeds are paid into the estate.

RRIF

The purpose of a Registered Retirement Income Fund (RRIF) is to pay an income stream from a RRSP. Annually you must withdraw at least a minimum amount of income as cash or in-kind, on a scale determined by a government, based upon the age of yourself--or your younger spouse if you so wish. If a RRIF is created by rollover of RRSP assets, the RRSP beneficiaries do not also roll; so, remember to make new beneficiary designations in the RRIF.[78] In Quebec, beneficiaries are named in your will or marriage contract and not In the RRIF unless purchased from a life Insurance company. To take advantage of the $2,000 pension income tax credit, you can roll some of your RRSP into a RRIF at age 65.

At your death, the full amount of the RRIF is included in your estate as taxable income but there are ways to defer taxes involving your spouse or dependants, to be discussed later in the chapters on support. The CRA holds both the estate and beneficiary jointly liable for any income tax due.[79]

If you are worried about RRIF income causing a clawback of Old Age Security payments, the "RRIF Meltdown" strategy can be used wherein

1. you obtain a loan,

---

[77] *Tax Guide T4040.*

[78] *ITA* s 146.3, IC78-18R6; *Bramley v Bramley,* 2003 CanLII 313 (BCSC).

[79] *ITA* s 160.2(2).

2. invest the loan in a non-registered portfolio geared to capital gains rather than income,

3. RRIF withdrawals pay the interest on the loan, and

4. interest payments on the loan are tax-deductible, and help to offset the tax on RRIF withdrawals.

This is an aggressive strategy that works best when markets are increasing in order to avoid capital losses on the loan's portfolio.

RRSP

A Registered Retirement Savings Plan (RRSP) encourages saving for retirement by permitting the deduction of plan contributions from taxable income up to the age of 71 when the contributions must be withdrawn as income or used to purchase an annuity or rolled into a RRIF or a combination of all three.[80]

At your death, the full amount of the RRSP is included in your estate as taxable income, although the named beneficiary receives the proceeds free of tax, which can be unfair to the residual beneficiaries of the estate. The CRA holds both the estate and beneficiary jointly liable for any income tax due.[81]

There are ways to defer the tax but differences exist whether the RRSP is unmatured (not yet making retirement payments) or matured (making payments) (see pp. 109, 114).[82]

A parent can control a child's RRSP by being named the irrevocable beneficiary such that changes cannot be made without the parent's approval.

---

[80]   *ITA s* 146.

[81]   *ITA s* 160.2(1).

[82]   *ITA ss* 60(l), 60.011, 60.02, 146(8.91); IT-500R; *CRA pamphlet RC4177.*

In Quebec, beneficiaries are named In your will or marriage contract and not in the RRSP unless purchased from a life insurance company.

A RRSP can be opened in the name of and owned by your spouse/ partner until age 71, to be known as a "**Spousal RRSP**." A contribution generates a tax credit for you (contributor) but also lowers your limit for contributions. If you are older than 71, or in the year of your death, contributions can still be made for the tax credit as long as you have contribution room.[83] If you contribute to a spousal RRSP and the money is withdrawn within 3 years, the income tax attribution rules will attribute the withdrawal back to you as taxable income.

TBP

A Target Benefit Plan (TBP) is a new alternative to a RPP and PRPP for an employee without a pension plan. The concept shares the investment risk of premiums between the employer and employee. Shortfalls in funding would be covered by a reduction in benefits or increase in contributions, either of which adversely impact the employee.

TBP is or will be available in some provinces[84] but not yet federally where it would apply to Crown corporations (eg. Canada Post) and privately to federally-regulated industries, such as banking, telecom, and transportation.

TFSA

A Tax Free Savings Account (TFSA) permits investments to grow tax-free and to be withdrawn tax-free but contributions are not tax-deductible.[85] Contribution room remains the same even though you can have more than one TFSA, similar to a RRSP. Withdrawals do not trigger clawbacks of income-tested government payments.

---

[83] *CRA Pamphlet P119* and *Guide T4040.*

[84] AB, BC, NB, NS, ON, QC.

[85] *ITA s* 146.2.

As a savings vehicle, a TFSA is preferred to a RRSP if:

- your income is not high enough to take advantage of the deductibility of a RRSP contribution,

- the pension adjustment on your RPP eats up your RRSP room,

- you anticipate a short-term need for the money,

- your income fluctuates and you need to make withdrawals in low income years,

- you want to continue contributions to a tax-sheltered program beyond age 71 (when contributions to a RRSP must end), or

- you do not want RRSP withdrawals (or eventual RRIF income) to cause clawbacks of government benefits, such as Old Age Security.

At your death, a beneficiary who is a spouse/partner can transfer the TFSA to her own TFSA without affecting her contribution room but other beneficiaries can transfer the TFSA only if they have sufficient contribution room; otherwise, the TFSA passes into your estate.[86] Pre-death (but not post-death) income and capital gains can be distributed tax-free to beneficiaries. A TFSA might not be so tax-free if you trade a lot in it as the CRA could consider your activity as carrying on a taxable business.

VRSP
A Voluntary Retirement Savings Plan (VRSP) is a PRPP in Quebec.[87]

---

[86]   *CRA "Death of a TFSA Holder."*

[87]   *Quebec Bill 39,* Dec. 3, 2013.

CHAPTER 8

TOOLS

PRODUCTS OF LIFE INSURANCE COMPANIES

Among the most useful tools used in estate planning are products of life insurance companies. At your death, they act as will-substitutes that your family can handle on their own by simply sending a death certificate to the insurance company. The payouts by the company are quick and can be outside your estate to beneficiaries, thereby avoiding probate,[88] or inside your estate to provide liquidity for estate gifts and liabilities.

8.1   Parties to a product

8.2   Life & other insurance

8.3   Segregated fund

8.4   Annuities

8.1   PARTIES TO A PRODUCT

Contract Owners (Single, Successor, Joint)
There are 4 parties to a product's contract:

- insurance company or "insurer",

---

[88]   *Higgins v R*, 2013 CanLII 194 (TCC);
Rozon Estate v Transamerica, [1999] OJ 4538 (OCA).

- contract owner (Quebec: "policyholder[89]),

- measuring life, and

- beneficiaries.

On the death of a single owner, the ownership passes to the owner's estate. If a successor owner is named (Quebec: "subrogated policyholder"), then ownership passes to the successor and nothing passes into the deceased's estate.

Care should be taken with joint ownership of a contract, whether tenants in common or joint tenants with right of survivorship, because the results may be unintended, as follows:

- if owners are joint tenants with right of survivorship, one owner is also annuitant, and both are beneficiaries, then if one dies, the proceeds will not be paid to the deceased's estate:

  1. if the annuitant dies, the contract ends, and the death benefit is paid to the surviving owner-beneficiary, but

  2. if the non-annuitant dies, the contract continues, the annuitant-owner takes ownership of the whole and becomes sole beneficiary for the death benefit, and

- if owners are tenants in common, one is annuitant, and both are beneficiaries, then

  1. if the annuitant dies, the contract ends, the death benefit is paid to the surviving owner-beneficiary and nothing passes to the deceased's estate, but

  2. if the non-annuitant dies, his ownership passes into his estate, the surviving annuitant-owner retains her ownership and becomes sole beneficiary for the whole death benefit.

---

[89]   *CCQ* c XV, Div II, arts 2415-2462, especially art 2445.

For spouse/partners, two alternatives are:

- two separate contracts, with one spouse/partner as owner/annuitant and the other as beneficiary, or

- one contract with one spouse/partner as owner and beneficiary, the other as annuitant and successor owner, and the children as contingent beneficiaries, so that:

  1. if the annuitant dies, the contract ends, the owner receives the death benefit as beneficiary,

  2. if the owner dies, ownership passes to the successor owner, the contract continues with the children as beneficiaries, and

  3. if both die, the children receive the proceeds as beneficiaries.

Measuring Life (Single, Successor, Joint Life)

The measuring life is generally called the "annuitant" but for life insurance is also called the "life insured."

A contract terminates on the death of a single annuitant but will continue if a successor annuitant has been named. The latter situation arises:

- if the owner is a corporation and wants a continuation of the contract, and

- between spouses if one is named as successor-owner and successor-annuitant.

A similar situation arises in life Insurance if a policy is joint first-to-die or last-to-die.

Beneficiaries

In addition to the common types of beneficiaries mentioned in chapter 2, you may encounter the "**family class,**" defined as:[90]

- in Quebec: the spouse/partner, ascendants, and descendants of the policyholder, and

- in the other provinces: the spouse/partner, parent, and (grand)child of the life insured.[91]

An owner Is not considered to be a beneficiary in the "family class", nor Is a trustee for a minor unless they are separately named.

If a family class is described as having a family class member and a non-member, the non-member's proceeds will be given to the member.[92] Before July 1962, the "family class" was known as "preferred beneficiaries."

If beneficiaries are described as "next-of-kin, heirs, assigns" or simply "estate", the insurance proceeds will be paid to the executor and pass through your estate subject to probate.

Remember that if you intend to name in your will a beneficiary of life insurance, then:

- identify the contract clearly, and

- ensure there are words included such as "and these proceeds shall not form part of my estate;"

otherwise, the proceeds may pass into instead of outside the estate thereby encountering probate. Remember that a naming of a beneficiary in your will can override an earlier designation in a contract;

---

[90]   eg. *IA* ss 191, 196; *Uniform Life Insurance Act*; *CCQ* arts 2456-2460.

[91]   Partner is included in most provinces except NB, NL, NU, SK, YT.

[92]   *Re Sutherland Estate* (1961), 27 DLR(2d) 166 (ABSC);
       Re Dunn, [1934] OWN 95 (HC); *Re Edwards* (1910), 22 OLR 367 (HC).

so, when drafting a will, check whether a designation in a contract is being overridden.

8.2 LIFE & OTHER INSURANCE

Life insurance is a contract where, in return for a periodic payment or premium, an insurer agrees to pay a fixed sum of money to a beneficiary named in the contract upon the death of a person whose life is insured.

Life insurance is useful in estate planning because growth within the policy is tax-sheltered, and the death benefit is paid tax-free.[93]

Dispositions of insurance policies prior to death, such as a surrender or loan, can produce taxable gains if the proceeds exceed the policy's cost base consisting of premiums paid less the pure cost of insurance. An assignment of a policy as collateral for a loan from a financial institution is not considered to be a taxable disposition. If the loan earns business or property income, then the interest on the loan can be tax-deductible.

There are generally two types of life insurance: permanent and term.

Permanent Life Insurance

Permanent life insurance is the traditional insurance that provides lifetime protection, a guaranteed basic death benefit, and a guaranteed cost of insurance. If it also participates in dividends declared by the insurer, then it is "participating insurance" and builds a cash value with tax-free growth.

There are a variety of types, but the more common are:

- Whole Life: premiums pay for insurance coverage and the excess builds up a cash value over time;

---

[93] *ITA* ss12.2, 20, 148; *IA* s 196(1); the federal 2014 budget proposes restrictions in 2017 for a tax-exempt policy regarding maximum premiums/deposits and cash value accumulations.

- Limited Payment Life: premiums are paid for a fixed term (eg. 20 yrs) or to age 65 and then no more premiums are due;

- Endowment Life: pays face value at death or at maturity;

- Joint First-to-Die: pays on first death;

- Joint Last-to-Die: pays on last death and is used to create an estate and to provide liquidity.

A newer type of permanent insurance is Universal Life or Variable Life wherein the policy owner decides on how the premiums are to be invested, unlike the above policies where the insurer makes the decisions. The owner can invest in the equity market whereas an insurer prefers the predictability of the bond market. Universal life has the flexibility of coverage, premium, and investments. It is often used when an owner has excess income or capital, wants tax-sheltered growth, and has maxed out his RRSP. More than one life, sometimes 5 lives, can be insured in the same policy.

Split Dollar or Shared Ownership Life Insurance

A joint ownership of a permanent life insurance policy is possible because the Income Tax Act refers to "interests" in a policy. The costs and benefits of a policy can be shared, called "split-receipting" by the CRA.[94] A formal legal agreement is made with:

1. the death benefit owner needing insurance coverage in the event of death,

2. the cash value owner wanting tax-sheltered growth represented by the cash surrender value of the policy,

3. both owners paying their respective portions of the premium, and

---

[94]   CRA Technical News No. 26 (Dec. 24, 2002) *Proposed Guidelines on Split-Receipting; ITA* s148(9) "adjusted cost base"; *Regu* 308.

4.   both owners naming a beneficiary to receive the proceeds of their portion of the life insurance policy when the life insured dies.

Term Life Insurance

Term life insurance provides protection for a specific period of time, usually 5, 10, or 20 years up to the age of 85 or less. A new Term-to-100 product now exists, which is really a non-participating permanent insurance policy to age 100. A term policy does not participate in dividends nor does it build up a cash value over time. Premiums are initially low and increase substantially at renewal time except for Term-to-100, which has no renewal.

The general purpose is to fund a short-term need (eg. mortgage, income loss) and, in the past, has not been appropriate for estate planning because, although cheap in the short term, renewals become costly. However, the Term-to-100 is a viable alternative.

Disability Insurance

Disability insurance protects your standard of living by providing an income replacement while you are unable to work. Disability insurance can be privately owned or supplied through a group plan by an employer. Disability payments through a group plan are generally taxable as income because the premiums are tax-deductible.

A privately-owned plan is different from a group plan in that it is usually portable, non-cancellable, has a cost-of-living adjustment, and definitions of disability are more favourable to the individual. Payments are also non-taxable because the premiums are not tax-deductible.

Critical Illness Insurance

Critical illness insurance protects a standard of living by providing a one-time lump sum payment in the event of a life-threatening disease (eg. heart attack, stroke, cancer). The lump sum can be invested for periodic income or to pay for accommodations, such as home renovations for wheelchair access. Payments are considered non-taxable.

Long Term Care Insurance

Long term care insurance covers the cost of a nursing home or in-home care when you cannot perform two activities of daily living: eating, bathing, dressing, toileting, transferring to and from a bed, and maintaining continence. Payments are considered non-taxable.

You will want to check the length of benefit period, benefit amount, and inflation protection. Policies can reimburse monthly expenses (less expensive) or provide a monthly amount regardless of expenses (more expensive).

8.3   SEGREGATED FUND

A segregated fund is a pool of investments kept separate or segregated from the general assets of the life insurance company. The fund operates like a mutual fund in that both are trusts and income and capital gains are flowed-through to the owner but, unlike a mutual fund:

- capital losses are also flowed-through to the owner,

- there is an important insurance component that acts as a capital guarantee at maturity (eg. every 15 years) and at death, to be treated as a capital gain if a top-up is paid,

- beneficiaries can be named,

- proceeds at decease are paid directly to beneficiaries outside the estate, thereby avoiding probate, and

- allocations to investors are not paid in cash like mutual fund distributions; for cash, a partial withdrawal is made.

The choice of annuitant is important because the guarantees are geared to the annuitant's life. The insurance component is an important feature because creditors, including the CRA, cannot seize the proceeds.[95] For a tax-free continuation of a non-registered contract, name a successor owner and successor annuitant, possibly your spouse/partner.

Some companies offer an option of guaranteed lifetime income which is attached to a segregated fund called a Guaranteed Minimum Withdrawal Benefit (GMWB). Payments are guaranteed even in the unlikely event that the investment's market value reduces to zero.

8.4 ANNUITIES

An annuity is a contract purchased with a sum of money that guarantees a future stream of income payments at regular intervals for a specified time or for a lifetime.

Payments are a blend of investment income and return of capital. For a purchase with non-registered funds, investment income is taxable but not the return of capital, which provides a higher income rate than a comparable GIC and helps to prevent a clawback of government benefits. For a purchase with registered funds, the entire payment is taxable. A taxable payment qualifies for the Pension Income Tax Credit.

Former drawbacks to annuities were inflexibility with no right to rescind the contract once signed. At your death, the company kept the capital and ended the contract. Times have changed with newer options for:

- a guarantee period in which benefits continue to a named beneficiary at your decease,

- a "refund" option if you die before your total income equals the original purchase price in which case your beneficiary or estate receives a lump sum ("cash refund") or continued payments ("installment refund"),

---

[95]   *Higgins v R*, 2013 CanLII194 (TCC).

- a "return of premium" option if you die before the first payment, and

- a "prescribed taxation" option to average out the taxable portion of payments over the life of a non-registered annuity.

Other advantages of an annuity are protection from creditors, decision-free investing, and the ability to name beneficiaries.

The following are the various types of annuities:

Accelerated or Impaired Annuity
Higher payments to cover care costs of a person with shortened life expectancy if aged 70 years or less.

Commutable Annuity
A registered annuity that can be surrendered in whole or in part at any time with a surrender charge. The cash value is transferable to another annuity or RRIF or taken as taxable income.

Deferred Annuity
The annuity is purchased now to lock in an interest rate and income payments are delayed to a future time, usually up to 15 years.

Indexed or Increasing Income Annuity
Income increases at a simple or compounded fixed rate.

Insured or Back-to-Back Annuity or Lifetime Term Deposit
A purchase of both an annuity and a life insurance policy to replenish the estate for funds used to purchase the annuity; funded only with non-registered monies.

Integrated Annuity

A bridge to retirement with early higher payments until government retirement benefits (CPP/QPP, OAS) commence; funded only with registered monies.

Level Income Annuity

A level guaranteed income for life.

Joint and Survivor Life Annuity

Lifetime income for you and your spouse/partner and can be combined with a guarantee period.

Prescribed Annuity

A non-registered annuity with payments having a consistent ratio of capital and income in order to average the amount of tax paid annually.[96]

Single Life Annuity

Lifetime income for you and can be combined with a guarantee period in case of early death.

Term Certain Annuity:

Income for a specified period of time, usually up to 30 years. If you die before the end of the term, a named beneficiary receives either a lump sum or continued payments.

Variable Annuity

Another name for a segregated fund with a value that fluctuates with the investment markets.

---

[96]   *ITA* ss 56(1)(d), 60(a); *Regu* 300, 304.

CHAPTER 9
TOOLS

TRUSTS: THE BASICS

9.1 Nature

9.2 How do you create a trust?

9.3 Trustee's Role

9.4 Variation

9.5 Rectification

9.6 Termination

9.7 Income Tax & Trusts

9.1 NATURE

A trust is a way for you to let another person handle some of your property in order to benefit a third person, such as a family member.

In Common Law, a trust is known as a "settlement" in which the property owner is a "settlor," the transfer is a settling of the property onto a "trustee" who holds legal title in the property for the benefit of a "beneficiary" who has beneficial title to income or capital or both.[97] There are two parts: the declaration of trust in which you (settlor) declare that the trustee holds property for beneficiaries, and secondly, your transfer of property to the trustee in trust.

---

[97] *Hardoon v Belilios*, [1901] A.C. 118 (P.C.), 123.

In Quebec Civil Law, there is no separation of legal and beneficial title and a trust is created by your transfer of property from a "patrimony" to a "trust patrimony" to be administered by a trustee for a particular purpose.[98] Much of the following discussion will be based on the Common Law concept of separation of ownership.

Trusts can be formal (written), informal (oral), or created by the law. Neither formality, writing, witnesses, nor a seal are necessary unless land is involved, in which case the trust must be in writing.[99] In Quebec, a trust must be formal and in writing.

A trust is sometimes confused with other things. A trust is not a "power", which is the authority (without a duty or ownership) to deal with property. A trust is not an "agency" because an agent is not an owner. A trust is not a legal entity because it cannot enter into contracts, purchase trust property, nor incur liabilities.

A trust can be costly to set up because there are initial legal costs, ongoing trustee and accounting fees, and the annual cost of preparing income tax returns.

Living v. Testamentary

You can set up a trust to take effect during your lifetime, called a "living" (latin:"inter vivos") trust, or it can be established in your will to be effective after death, known as a "testamentary" trust.

In income tax, a testamentary trust is one that arises on or as a consequence of your death.[100] An "estate" is considered to be a testa-

---

[98]   CCQ, arts 1260-1265.

[99]   eg. *Statute of Frauds*, RSO. c S.19.

[100]   *ITA* ss 108(1), 248(9.1).

mentary trust.[101] A trust will lose its testamentary status for income tax and become a living trust if:[102]

1. property is contributed by anyone other than you, such as by a joint owner or by a living trust, but not if the property arises from:

   - a purchase at fair market value,

   - another testamentary trust or will as a gift or forgiveness of a debt,

   - a beneficiary's disclaimer (before acceptance) of an interest in the trust but not a release or surrender,

   - insurance proceeds on your life, or

   - a beneficiary foregoing a payment before it is payable;

2. the trust incurs a debt to a beneficiary (but not if paying for services rendered to the trust or reimbursing for expenses paid on behalf of the trust);

3. the trust pays a debt guaranteed by a beneficiary to a non-arm's length person (a person not bargaining independently);

4. a trustee prolongs a distribution of an estate; or

5. beneficiary interests are varied.

As of 2016, there are three different testamentary trusts: ordinary (and pre-2016), GRE (graduated rate estate), and QDT (qualified

---

[101]   *ITA* ss104(1), (2), 108(1), 248(1) "trust"; *Grayson v MNR* (2000), 90 DTC 1108 (TCC).

[102]   *ITA* s108(1) "testamentary trust", 248(9) "disclaimer" CRA "Types of Trusts"; *Greenberg Estate v The Queen* (1997), 97 DTC 1380 (TCC). *Biderman v The Queen*, 2000 CanLII 14987 (FCA).

disability trust).[103] The first is taxed at a top rate, the second at a graduated rate for 3 years and then a top rate, and the third at a graduated rate. The tax can be avoided by paying income to beneficiaries who are taxed. A testamentary trust remains useful to control the frequency and amount of payments to beneficiaries, to avoid creditors, to manage money for a minor, and to protect assets for remainder interests.

9.2 HOW DO YOU CREATE A TRUST?

You will probably need the services of a lawyer to draw up a formal document or to put the trust into your will. The lawyer can tell you that there are three conditions, known as the "Three Certainties:" **Intent, Subject-Matter, and Objects (Beneficiaries)**.[104]

Intent

You must have a clear intention to create a trust which you can state expressly or imply from your conduct. The usual express words are "in trust" or "as trustee for." No trust will be created if you have mere discussions, a wish, a hope[105] or you retain control over your property,[106] or you really intended to give the property away as a gift.[107]

---

[103] *ITA* ss 122(1)(3); top tax rate is 33%.

[104] *Kingsdale Securities v MNR* (1974), 28 DTC 6674 (FCA); *Henfrey v Samson Belair*, [1989] 2 SCR 24. *Anspor Con struction v Neuberger* 2016 CanLII 75 (ONSC).

[105] *Bell v Bell Estate* (1999), 24 ETR (2d) 38 (BCSC) *Bank of Montreal v Bower* (1889), 18 OR 226 (Ch) *Atinco Paper v The Queen* (1978), 32 DTC 6387 (FCA) *Galt Paper v MNR* (1978), 32 DTC 6406 (FCA).

[106] *Duca Financial v Bozzo*, 2011 CanLII 455 (ONCA); *Carson v.Wilson*, 1960 CanLII 104 (OCA).

[107] *Re Hordynsky*, 1983 CanLII 2027 (SKQB)

Subject-Matter

You must be clear as to the portion of your property for each beneficiary and when the beneficiary is to receive it. The property must be capable of transfer, correct formalities (if any) must be observed (eg. real estate deed), and an actual transfer must occur. Two legal rules are encountered: the Rule Against Perpetuities and the Rule Against Accumulations.

To prevent a trust from continuing indefinitely, the Common Law created the Rule Against Perpetuities, which states that the subject-matter must be transferred to beneficiaries within a "Perpetuities Period," meaning "a life in being + 21 years," although some provinces have a "wait & see" position,[108] others have abolished the Rule,[109] and P.E.I. has extended the period to 60 years. The rule does not exist in Quebec.

Similarly, the "Rule Against Accumulations" states that income can only remain in the trust for the Perpetuity Period before being paid out. This Rule has been abolished in some provinces.[110]

Objects (Beneficiaries)

The beneficiaries can be people or purposes, they must be known or determinable, and the beneficial interest in the property can be transferred or is conditional on an event.

For the test of beneficiaries being known or determinable, they can be identified by name, class, or group for which an examination would be made of your intentions and the earliest time for distribution (or a court order to make a distribution).[111]

---

[108]   AB, BC, NT, ON.

[109]   SK, MB, NS.

[110]   AB, BC, MB, SK.

[111]   *Kingsdale Securities v MNR* (1974), 28 DTC 6674 (FCA).

For the test of the beneficial interest being transferred or contingent, the beneficiaries must be ascertainable and known as in "to A when he reaches 21," or conditional as in "to A if he survives me," but not where unknown as in "to executors to distribute as they see fit."[112]

9.3 TRUSTEE'S ROLE

Taking on the role of trustee is not an easy task. The trustee has various powers but also obligations. Furthermore, the liability of a trustee is personal based on ownership of trust property and there is no right of indemnity from the beneficiaries.[113] In regard to third parties, the liability is limited to the value of the trust property.

The trustee's powers are:

- to deal with property,

- to determine the distribution date of the trust,

- to determine beneficiaries (if not already done so),

- to encroach on capital,

- to distribute income and capital to beneficiaries, unequally if allowed, and

- to appoint a replacement trustee.

A trustee has obligations:

- to disclose to beneficiaries matters affecting the trust;[114]

- to act personally and not to delegate duties although agents can be used;[115]

---

[112]   *Daniels v Daniels Estate*, 1991 CanLII 288 (ABCA).

[113]   *Wagner v van Cleef*, 1991 CanLII 7168 (OCGD Div).

[114]   *Re Ballard Estate*, 1994 CanLII 7305 (OCGD).

[115]   *Wagner v Van Cleef*, 1991 CanLII 7168 (OCGD Div).

- to act in the best interest of beneficiaries, but otherwise only if the beneficiaries consent and any action taken is fair and honest;[116]

- to act only by unanimous decision if numbering more than one;

- to exercise the standard of care and diligence expected of a reasonable and prudent person in conducting their own affairs;[117] which standard is higher for a professional trustee or trust company;[118] known as the "prudent Investor rule;"

- to act with an "even hand" among beneficiaries, between the income and capital recipients, and between a life tenant and the remainder interests;[119] and

- to avoid a conflict of interest, or a personal profit or a benefit from the trust.

The beneficiaries can compel a trustee to observe and to perform his obligations.[120]

9.4 VARIATION

Sometimes a trust needs to be changed or varied after it has been created. Variation can occur through terms in the trust, or

---

[116]   *Nat. Trust Co.Ltd. v Osadchuk*, [1943] SCR 89.

[117]   *Fales v Canada Permanent Trust*, [1977] 2 SCR 302.

[118]   Re Waterman's Will Trusts, [1952] 2 All ER 1054 (Ch.).

[119]   *Re Smith*, 1971 CanLII 577 (OCA);
        Cheadle v Mayotte (1995), 7 ETR(2d) 167 (OCGD);
        Edell v Sitzer, 2001 CanLII 27989 (OSC);
        Martin v Banting, 2002 CanLII 13032 (OCA).

[120]   *Re Proniuk, 1984 CanLII 1337 (ABQB).*

by provincial legislation,[121] or by agreement of all beneficiaries.[122] Generally, a court is reluctant to approve a variation and will look at the following tests:[123]

- if there is a class of persons, each must benefit,

- there is consistency with your original intention or the mere filling-in of a gap in your intention,

- the variation does not affect the entire trust, and

- consent can be given for persons unascertained, incapable, unborn, or those subject to a discretionary power,[124] but consent cannot be given if detrimental to those incapable of consenting, nor for a competent adult beneficiary who does not consent or cannot be found.[125]

Be careful of income tax consequences of a variation.[126] Generally a taxable disposition is not considered to have occurred unless a fundamental change has been made, in which case a new trust will

---

[121]   *Trustee Act* in the provinces of AB, MB, NB:

　　　　RSA 1980, c T-10; RSM 1987 c T-160, s 59; RSNB 1973, c T-15, s 26

　　　　Variation of Trusts Act in the provinces of NS, NT, ON, PE, SK, YT:

　　　　RSNS 1989, c 486; RSNWT 1988, c V.1; RSO 1990, c V.1; RSPEI 1988, c V-1; RSS 1978, c V-1; RSY 1986, c 174.

　　　　Lastly, BC--> *Trust and Settlement Variation Act,* RSBC 1996, c 463.

[122]   Rule of *Saunders v Vautier* (1841) 49 ER 282 (Ch.); Also called the "Doctrine of Acceleration". Abolished in AB & MB.

[123]   *Eaton v Eaton-Kent ,* 2013 CanLII 7985 (ONSC);

　　　　Re Davies, 1967 CanLII 255 (OSC);

　　　　Finnell v Schumacher Estate, 1990 CanLII 6766 (OCA).

[124]   *Russ v British Columbia (Public Trustee),* 1994 CanLII 1730 (BCCA);

　　　　Leir v B.C. Public Trustee, 1983 CanLII 597 (BCSC).

[125]   *Chapman v Chapman,* [1954] 1 All ER 798 (HL).

[126]   *ITA* s 107(2).

be deemed to have been created. For example, a fundamental change might allow the income beneficiary to access capital. Variation might also trigger attribution rules. A mere change of trustees or their powers is not considered a fundamental change.

9.5 RECTIFICATION

Similar to a will, a rectification changes a trust to achieve what you intended as in the case of a clerical error, a misunderstanding of instructions, or a failure to carry out instructions.[127] Your intention in creating the trust should be clear.[128] A rectification cannot be an amendment.

9.6 TERMINATION

A trust may be terminated by:

- express terms in the trust deed,

- fulfillment of the trust,

- court order or operation of the law, such as for fraud on creditors,

- your retention of the power to revoke the trust, or

- all of the beneficiaries agree to terminate.[129]

If a beneficiary is unascertained or incapable, a court can provide consent.[130] If there is a "gift over" (condition subsequent) then the gift passes to another beneficiary to avoid the problems of consent.

---

[127] *Attorney General of Canada v Juliar*, 2000 CanLII 16883 (OCA);
Jean Coutu Group v Canada, 2016 SCC 55 (CanLII)
Canada v Fairmont Hotels, 2016 SCC 56 (CanLII).

[128] *Rose v Rose*, 2006 CanLII 20856 (OSC).

[129] Rule of *Saunders v Vautier* (1841), 49 ER 282 (Ch.).

[130] *Russ v British Columbia (Public Trustee)*, 1994 CanLII 1730 (BCCA).

If the trust is irrevocable, you cannot get your assets back unless the beneficiaries consent.

9.7   INCOME TAX & TRUSTS

Taxable Entity

A trust is considered to be a taxable individual separate from you and the trustee.[131] Multiple trusts for one individual or class are grouped to be one trust but are acceptable if made irrevocably for several persons individually.[132] Similar to a will, the residence of a trust depends on the location of its central management and control.[133]

Living trusts are taxed at the top rate. As for the three testamentary trusts: ordinary (and pre-2016), GRE (graduated rate estate), and QDT (qualified disability), the 1st is taxed at the top rate, the 2nd at a graduated rate for 3 years and then at the top rate, and the 3rd at a graduated rate.[134]

Transfers-in of Property

The transfer of property to a trust can have income tax consequences. A deemed disposition will occur:

- at fair market value if the transfer is a gift or there is no change of beneficial ownership, and

- at fair market value to the transferor and at cost to the transferee if the transfer is below fair market value or at non-arm's length (persons not bargaining independently).[135]

---

[131]   *ITA* s 104(2).

[132]   *ITA* s 104(2); *Mitchell v MNR* (1956), 10 DTC 521 (TAB).

[133]   *ITF-S6-F1-C1; Fundy Settlement v Canada*, 2012 CanLII 14 (SCC). *Herman Grad 2000 Family Trust v Minister of Revenue*, 2016 CanLII 2402, 2407 (ONSC).

[134]   *ITA* s 122(1)(3); top tax rate is 33% for 2016.

[135]   *ITA* ss 69(1)(b)(c), 74.1-74.5, 75, 251; *ITF-S1-F5-C1*.

Exceptions to the tax consequences are the following transfers:

- rollovers, such as to an alter ego, joint partner, self-benefit or spousal trust,[136]

- rollover to a testamentary trust for qualified farming, fishing or small business,[137]

- cash or equivalent,[138]

- trust-to-trust transfer,

- inside some registered products (eg. RRSP), or

- payment of debt or to secure an obligation.

Payments-out

Beneficiaries can receive income or capital or both, depending on the trust.

The term "income" can cause confusion because it has different meanings in trust and tax law. In trust law, income is interest and dividends but not capital gains whereas all three are income for income tax. If income is to be generated by investing the capital in a mutual fund, then a problem may arise if the payment stream requires a redemption of fund units. The fund units are "capital" in trust law to which the income beneficiary would not be entitled and would end up receiving a smaller amount than anticipated.

---

[136] *ITA* ss 73(1.01), 107.4, IT-325R2.

[137] *ITA* ss 70(9)-(9.11); IT-349R3.

[138] *ITA* ss 40, 69.

The attribution rules can also be a problem unless the transfer to the trust is at fair market value.[139] Income and capital gains can be attributed back from a beneficiary to you (settlor) in several ways:[140]

- if the trust is revocable (but not if irrevocable),

- if the trust pays income to a minor (but not if the trust is testamentary or providing necessities of life),

- if you retain control over the property, such as determining trustees or distributions or requiring your consent, or

- if trust property will revert to you, such as by a lack of beneficiaries.

Formerly, a payment to a beneficiary could be taxable either in the trust or at the beneficiary, depending on which had the lower tax rate. but as of 2016 the tax is payable by the beneficiary.[141] Capital losses cannot be passed out to beneficiaries.[142] Personal tax credits and elections are not available to a trust.[143]

If the beneficiaries will be paying the tax, then the payment is simply a flow-through from the trust.[144] Dividends and capital gains retain their character but not active business income.[145] Payments for a

[139]   *The Queen v Sommerer*, 2012 CanLII 207 (FCA).

[140]   *ITA* ss 74.1-74.5, 75, 75.2, 107(4.1), IT-369R, 369RSR S.R.;
        Degrace Family Trust v The Queen, 1998 CanLII 336 (TCC).

[141]   *ITA* ss 104(13.3), 106(1.1); *Lussier v The Queen*, 1999 CanLII 329 (TCC).

[142]   *ITA* ss 104(13.1), (13.2).

[143]   *ITA* s 122(1.1).

[144]   *ITA* ss 104(6), (13).

[145]   *ITA* ss 104(19), (21).

minor are made to a parent or guardian.[146] If the beneficiary disclaims the gift before receiving any benefit, then there is no taxable event for the beneficiary; however, a release or surrender by the beneficiary may be taxable because it occurs after acceptance of the gift.[147]

A trustee should be given discretion to enable the distribution of income to the lower tax-bracket beneficiaries and also discretion to determine the income and capital portions of a payment. Income not distributed is added to the capital of the trust.

Dispositions

A transfer of an <u>income</u> interest in a trust is a taxable distribution at fair market value.

A disposition of <u>capital</u> property is deemed to occur at fair market value.[148] However, a rollover is available for a disposition from a personal trust to your spouse/partner while you are alive and to a capital beneficiary after your death.[149] If the attribution rules have applied at some time to the trust, then the rollover is limited to your spouse/partner. An election out of the rollover on a property-by-property basis is available and would be done if there are no capital gains on some property or if there are offsetting capital losses or exemptions.[150]

The "principal residence exemption" (chapter 18) can be preserved by a beneficiary who is using the property as a principal residence.

---

[146]   *Langer Family Trust v MNR* (1992), 46 DTC 1055 (TCC)

[147]   *ITF-S6-F2-C1; Biderman v The Queen*, 2000 CanLII 14987 (FCA).

[148]   *ITA* s 107(2.1).

[149]   *ITA* s 107(2).

[150]   *ITA* ss 70(6.2), (6.3); 107(2.001).

Trusts for such purposes are a personal trust,[151] a spousal trust, an alter ego or joint partner trust, and of course, a principal residence trust.

Additionally, a living trust avoids a deemed disposition on death and is not part of an estate, which is useful for privacy and to avoid probate. Using a will to distribute trust property will trigger probate.

The Income Tax Act deems a taxable disposition of capital property every 21 years to avoid the perpetual deferral of tax on capital gains.[152] The 21-year period runs from the date of formation of the trust, with the exception that it runs from the date of death of you or your spouse/partner for a trust that is spousal, alter ego, joint partner, or self-benefit, as the case may be. The Rule does not apply to deferred income trusts, such as a RRSP, RRIF, and RESP,[153] nor to non-capital property, such as life insurance held In an insurance trust. The 21-year rule is often avoided for a personal trust by distributing trust assets to the trust's capital beneficiaries on a rollover basis but not to another trust, which merely inherits the former trust's disposition day.[154]

[151]   *ITA* ss107 (2.01), 40(4), 70(6), 73(1).

[152]   *ITA* ss104(4)-(5.2).

[153]   *ITA* ss 108(1) "trust" (a)-(g).

[154]   *ITA* ss 104(4)-(5.8), 107(2).

CHAPTER 10

TOOLS

TRUSTS: THE TYPES
(Alphabetically)

Although there are many types of trusts, basically "a trust is a trust" and the types merely reflect the use to which they are put. The following trusts can be living or testamentary, unless stated otherwise. The disadvantages of trusts is their setup costs with a lawyer and their ongoing maintenance costs of accounting and income tax returns.

In Quebec, there are three types of trusts:

- "social" for community purposes, such as a charitable trust,

- "personal" to benefit a person, and

- "private" for a specific use or purpose.

The balance of this chapter deals with trusts outside Quebec.

Age 40 Trust ("Fixed Allocation Trust")

You use this trust to retain a beneficiary's trust income until payout at a pre-determined age, although it doesn't have to be 40.[155] If the beneficiary is a minor, the income can be taxed at the minor's graduated rate.

Alter Ego Trust

If you want your property to go to named beneficiaries at your death and to avoid probate but, until then, you want to keep using your property, then an alter ego trust is helpful.

This is a living trust in which you must be aged 65 or older, the sole beneficiary, and you are the only person with access to the income and capital.[156] You can also be trustee. You and the trust must be Canadian residents.

A transfer-in of property does not trigger a capital gain because of a tax-deferred rollover of property to the trust.[157] An election can be made not to use the rollover if there are offsetting capital losses, exemptions, or tax credits.[158]

At your death, probate is avoided because your assets pass to named beneficiaries and not to your estate; however, income taxes are due by the trust from a deemed disposition at fair market value.[159] Income tax rollovers, such as to your spouse/partner, are not allowed. The income tax cannot be offset by life insurance owned by the trust on you because other beneficiaries would thereby benefit from the

---

[155] *ITA* s 104(18).

[156] *ITA* ss 73(1.01)(c)(ii); 104 (4)(a)(iv)(A), 248(1).

[157] *ITA* ss 73(1), (1.01)(c)(ii).

[158] *ITA* ss104(4)(a)(ii.1), (b), (c).

[159] *ITA* ss 104(2), (4); although new 104(13.4) implies the estate now pays.

capital. The principal residence exemption is available.[160] The 21-year deemed disposition rule does not apply until your death.[161] If a new trust is created at your death, it will be living and not testamentary.

The advantages of the trust for you are:

- retention, use, and control of your property,

- an alternative to a power of attorney,

- avoidance of probate, claims,[162] and variation of wills,

- avoidance of land transfer tax because beneficial ownership does not change,

- deferral of income tax,

- deferral of the 21-year disposition rule, and

- confidentiality (by avoiding probate).

The disadvantages are:

- only the transfer of capital property is tax-deferred, not resource property, raw land, goodwill, inventory, insurance products, registered products (eg. RRSP, RRIF), which transfer at fair market value,[163]

- other taxes are not necessarily avoided, such as GST/HST,[164]

---

[160]   *ITA* s 40(4).

[161]   *ITA* ss 104(4)(a.4), 108(1) "trust" (g)(i).

[162]   *Mawdsley v Nesen*, 2012 CanLII 91 (BCCA).

[163]   *ITA* ss 146(1), (12)(a).

[164]   *Excise Tax Act*, s 268.

- any income or loss or capital gain or loss is attributed back to you for taxation,[165]

- unavailability of the following when you die:

    - personal deductions,

    - exemptions and rollovers for qualified farming, fishing, and small business, and the spousal rollover,

    - capital losses in the estate to offset gains in the trust, and vice versa,

    - carry back of losses, and

- lack of creditor protection in the event of your bankruptcy.

Some people view an insurance segregated fund as an alternative to the trust with continuing control of assets, naming of beneficiaries, avoiding probate, confidentiality, and minimal costs of setup and maintenance.

Asset Protection Trust

You would use this trust when you want:

- to protect your assets or your estate from claims of creditors or dependants, or from an equalization payment to your spouse (discussed in chapter 12), or

- to leave a valuable asset, like a principal residence, to children of an earlier marriage and not to your current spouse/partner.

The trustee should have full discretion in the distribution of income and capital.

---

[165] *ITA* s 75(2).

Bare Trust ("Naked, Simple, or Dry" Trust)

You use this trust when you want the trustee to follow instructions passively in distributing trust property to the beneficiaries.[166] However, if you are also the beneficiary then, for income tax purposes, the relationship is considered to be an agency and not a trust, because beneficial title has not been transferred.

Charitable Trust

You create this tax-exempt trust to benefit a charity with the exclusive purposes of the relief of poverty, advancement of education or religion, or activities beneficial to the community.[167] If necessary, the "Certainty of Objects" can be supplied by a court.[168]

Charitable Remainder Trust

You set up this trust as a living trust when you want to receive a lifetime income from your property and, at your death, pass it to a charity or you can set it up in your will to pay a lifetime income to a beneficiary and, at his death, the property passes to the charity. There must not be the ability of yourself or the income beneficiary to encroach on the assets.

You transfer property into the trust, retain a life interest, and make an irrevocable gift of the residual interest to a registered charity which issues a tax receipt (see Chapter 20.7).[169]

---

[166]   *ITA* ss 69(1)(b)(iii), 104(1), (1.1), 108(1) "trust";
    Peragine v The Queen, 2012 CanLII 348 (TCC);
    Trident Holdings Ltd. v Danand Investments Ltd., 1988 CanLII 194 (OCA).

[167]   *ITA* ss149(1)(f), 149.1"charitable organization"; *Tax Guide* T4063;
    Income Tax Commrs. v Pemsel, [1891] AC 531 (HL).

[168]   *Jones v T. Eaton Co.,* 1973 CanLII 14 (SCC).

[169]   *Charitable Remainder Trust,* CRA, CSP-C02.

Constructive Trust

The courts create this trust when there has been an "unjust enrichment" of one person at the expense of another either:

- without any legal justification (eg. without a gift, contract, or statutory obligation),[170] or

- by trespass, crime, or breach of a duty owed to the person.[171]

The "Certainty of Intention" is supplied by the court and you allege that the holder of the property is holding in trust for you or another person.[172] Corroboratory evidence may be required if you are dead.[173] The trust is not taxable until its existence is found by a court.[174]

Dependants' Relief Trust

A trust created by the courts based on moral obligations found in provincial legislation dealing with dependant's relief.[175]

Disability Trust, Qualified Disability Trust (QDT)

A disability trust is a living trust created by you with provincial approval and monitoring to make payments to a disabled person for purposes such as education. The value of the trust cannot exceed $100,000 and any excess could offset provincial disability payments. Income not paid out to the beneficiary is deemed to be received

---

[170]   *Peter v Beblow*, 1993 CanLII 126 (SCC);
         Becker v Pettkus, 1980 CanLII 22 (SCC);
         Garland v Consumers Gas Co, 2004 CanLII 25 (SCC).

[171]   *Soulos v Korkontzilas*, 1997 CanLII 346 (SCC);
         International Corona Resources v Lac Minerals, 1989 CanLII 34 (SCC).

[172]   *Johnstone v Johnstone* (1913), 12 DLR 537 (OCA).

[173]   eg. *Ontario Evidence, Act*. RSO 1990, c. E.23.

[174]   *Fletcher v MNR* (1987), 41 DTC 624 (TCC).

[175]   *ITA* s 248(9.1).

anyway. Income accumulated in the trust may be taxed at the highest marginal rate because it is a living trust.

The Qualified Disability Trust (QDT) was created by the federal 2014 budget. The trust is testamentary and, unlike other trusts, will continue to enjoy a graduated income tax rate after 2015. The disabled person is the trust beneficiary who must qualify for the Disability Income Tax Credit.[176]

Discretionary Trust
A trust in which you give to your trustee a power of choosing how to operate the trust, such as the timing and amount of payments to beneficiaries. Your non-binding memorandum or letter of wishes helps to avoid beneficiary disputes as to the exercise of discretion.

Family Trust
You set up this trust to make clear how your assets are to be handled and divided among family members. The beneficiaries can be your current or former spouse/partners, and children of current and former marriages. Assets, like a family business, can be transferred to the trust but not on a tax-deferred basis. Proceeds often come from a life insurance policy on you. Your trustee is usually given discretion on payments to beneficiaries.

Graduated Rate Estate (GRE)
A testamentary trust during its first 36 months, if so elected. During the 36 months it enjoys a graduated rate of income tax.

Henson Trust
If you want to give income or assets to a disabled person without affecting provincial disability payments, then you would use a Henson

[176] *ITA* ss 122(1)-(3).

Trust.[177] Your trustee is given absolute discretion in making payments and the disabled person is the beneficiary who has no right to demand trust money, no control, and is deemed not to have received the trust income nor capital. The trust is not available in some provinces.[178]

The trustee's discretion must be absolute, such as:

"to pay income and capital In their absolute and unfettered discretion...income and capital shall not vest in [beneficiary]"

Do not use words of direction, such as "for his support, maintenance, and education"[179] because they fetter discretion.

In regard to taxes, there is no limit on assets sheltered nor limit on uses (eg. disability, education) but there is no tax-deferred rollover on assets transferred to the trust; so, income tax will be due on the transfer. The assets should not be transferred to the disabled person. Payments should be taxed in the hands of the disabled person who will probably have a rate of income tax lower than the trust. A payment need not be actually transferred if the amount can be considered "payable" or "paid" to the disabled person but remain in the trust under a "preferred beneficiary election."[180]

Inheritance Trust

Provincial disability payments could also be lost if a disabled person receives a large inheritance from someone's estate. As long as the inheritance does not exceed $100,000, it can be placed into an inheritance trust with discretion in the trustee to make payments to

---

[177]   *Ontario v Henson* (1988), 28 ETR 121 (OSC Div); (1989), 36 ETR 192 (OCA); *ITA ss* 60(1), 60.01, 104(14), IT-394R2.

[178]   AB, NT, NU; NL if over $100,000.

[179]   *Ozad v Ontario,* [1998] OJ 6498 (Div.Ct.).

[180]   *ITA* ss 104(14), 108(1).

the disabled person who, again, has no control over the trust and no right to demand payment.

Informal Trust ("In Trust For" or ITF)

This informal trust is opened as an account at a financial institution, often by a parent who wants a child to gain experience in the financial markets. The parent opens and puts money into the account and the child as beneficiary makes investment choices (probably with the parent's help). A problem is that the income attribution rules may apply to attribute any income back to the parent but not capital gains if the child Is a minor.[181] The trust does not exist in Quebec where trusts must be formal.

Joint Partner Trust

If you want to arrange for your property to go to named beneficiaries without probate after both you and your spouse/partner are dead but, until then, both of you want to keep using your property, then a joint partner trust is helpful.

Yes, it does look a lot like the alter ego trust because:

- there is a tax-deferred rollover of property to the trust,

- you and your spouse/partner are the beneficiaries,

- you and your spouse/partner have sole access to the income and capital,[182]

- you must be at least age 65 (but not your spouse/partner),

- you and the trust must be Canadian residents, and

---

[181]   *ITA* ss 56(2)-(4.3), 74.1-74.5, 75(2), 75.1.

[182]   *ITA* ss 73(1.02), 104(4)(a)(iv)(A), (13); 74.1(1), 74.2(1).

- the advantages and disadvantages are the same as the alter ego trust.[183]

However, the attribution rules attribute trust income and taxable capital gains received by the spouse/partner back to you while you are alive.

The trust survives both you and your spouse/partner as a living trust, passes to the named beneficiaries and not to your estates such that probate is avoided; however, income taxes are due by the trust from a deemed disposition at fair market value.[184] The trust survives divorce. The 21-year deemed disposition rule does not apply until both of you are dead at which point the trust continues as a living trust.[185]

Life Insurance Trust

You purchase life insurance on yourself and make a declaration of the existence of a trust that will receive the insurance proceeds upon your death. The declaration can be in your will or in the insurance contract referencing a trust in your will, but the best way to avoid probate is a separate trust agreement or trust deed.[186]

At your death, the proceeds go directly to the trust and not into your estate. The declaration should identify the insurance company, policy number, trustee, and beneficiaries.[187] The executor can be the trustee but not a beneficiary. Multiple insurance trusts for multiple

---

[183]   *ITA* ss 73(1.01)(c)(iii); 104(4)(a)(ii.1)(iii)(iv); 146(1), (12)(a).

[184]   *ITA* ss 104(4), although new 104(13.4) implies the estate now pays.

[185]   *ITA* ss 104(4), 108(1) "trust" (g)(i).

[186]   eg. IA s 193.

[187]   *Sun Life v Taylor*, 2008 CanLII 403 (SKQB); *Carlisle Estate*, 2007 CanLII 435 (QB).

beneficiaries are allowed. The insurance company should be notified of the trust.

The trust is considered testamentary even though the terms of the trust are established while you are alive and the proceeds come from a third party. The CRA regards the trust as testamentary because it arises on or as a consequence of death on condition that you are both the policyowner and life insured.[188] Similarly, a joint insurance policy should be joint-last-to-die in order for the trust to rely upon death, which is not the case with a joint-first-to-die policy.

Care should be taken in naming beneficiaries, because if an insurance trust is set up in the will, and a beneficiary designation in the policy is changed at some later date without mention of the trust, the later designation prevails and the insurance trust in the will fails. A revocation of a will revokes a trust in it but the invalidation of a will does not necessarily revoke the trust.[189]

Lifetime Benefit Trust

This is a discretionary trust in your will that resembles a Henson trust set up to support a mentally infirm and dependent spouse/partner or (grand)child who alone can receive the income and capital of the trust.[190]

Non-Charitable Purpose Trust

This trust looks like a charitable trust but not all of its purposes are charitable, such as the maintenance of graves or pets. In the past,

---

[188]   *ITA* ss 70(5), (6.1), 108(1); *Kingsdale Securities v MNR (1974)*, 28 DTC 6674 (FCA).

[189]   eg. IA s192.

[190]   *ITA* s 60.011(1), CRA "Types of Trusts."

this trust used to offend the 21-year Rule Against Perpetuities, but amendments have now remedied the problem.[191]

Non-Resident Immigration Trust

The 2014 federal budget proposed to eliminate this trust but, until now, if you were an immigrant to Canada, you could avoid Canadian income tax for 5 years on "foreign source income" (income outside Canada) as long as it was sheltered in the trust and not distributed to you.[192] Income accumulated in the trust could be paid tax-free as capital. The trust was created before entering Canada with the majority of trustees non-resident. Probate was avoided. After the 5-year period, the trust was subject to Canadian tax.

Non-Resident (Offshore) Trust

A topic worthy of its own book. Traditionally, taxes on payments from a non-resident offshore trust to you, a Canadian resident, were assumed to have been paid by the trust in its offshore jurisdiction. The trust added the income to capital and sent the funds to you in Canada as capital. Assuming the offshore jurisdiction had no taxation, there would be no tax to the trust nor to the Canadian recipient.

Generally, the CRA views such a trust to be a taxable Canadian resident if its contributor and beneficiary are Canadian residents. A Canadian beneficiary is liable for the tax owing.[193] A proposed federal change intends to make the trust taxable if its contributor or beneficiary are Canadian resident.

---

[191]   eg. *Perpetuities Act*, s 16; Waters, D., Gillen, M., Smith, L., *Law of Trusts in Canada* 4th ed. (Toronto: Thomson Carswell: 2012). at 627.

[192]   *ITA* s 94.

[193]   *ITA* ss 248(25); 94; Parliament's Ways and Means Motion 24/10/12.

Percentage Trust

This trust permits a trustee to avoid a distinction between income and capital beneficiaries.[194] The whole of the trust funds can be invested for a maximum return without the need to keep an "even hand" between income and capital beneficiaries. A beneficiary receives periodically a percentage of the trust's fair market value.

Personal Trust

In this trust all of the beneficiaries receive their interests as gifts.[195] All testamentary trusts and most family trusts are personal trusts. Nothing is paid for property contributed to the trust. A testamentary personal trust is now called a Graduated Rate Estate.

Capital property can be distributed at cost by a tax-deferred rollover to a capital beneficiary but this may change with federal budgets.[196] Care must be taken to avoid the application of the attribution rules that can nullify the tax-deferred rollover, especially where the capital property transferred can revert to you (the "reversionary trust rule").[197]

The trust can be used to receive capital property transferred out of another trust on a tax-deferred basis to avoid the 21-year income tax rule.[198] Another use has been to hold a home that qualifies as a principal residence (chapter 18) that is ordinarily occupied by a beneficiary of the trust or spouse or child of the beneficiary.[199]

---

[194]   *Primo Poloniato Grandchildren's Trust v Browne*, 2012 CanLII 862 (ONCA).

[195]   *ITA* s 248(1) "personal trust."

[196]   *ITA* s107(2).

[197]   *ITA* ss 75(2), 107(4.1).

[198]   *ITA* ss107(2), 248(1).

[199]   *ITA* ss 54(c.1), 107(2.01), 248(1); *ITF-S1-F3-C2*.

Pet Trust
A non-charitable purpose trust for the care and maintenance of a pet.[200]

Principal Residence Trust
A trust designed to hold title to a principal residence (chapter 18) for a beneficiary. You use the principal residence exemption to avoid income tax on the transfer and the trustee should make the necessary CRA filings to maintain the exemption. The trust must be an alter ego trust, spousal trust, joint partner trust, a self-benefit trust, or a qualified disability trust but, if not, a rollover is possible to an occupying beneficiary who can claim the exemption (ITA 107(2), (2.01), (2.001)).

Protective Trust
A trust to which you transfer property on a tax-deferred rollover basis with no change in beneficial ownership and only you have access to the income and capital.[201] It is often used where the health of you or a beneficiary is deteriorating.

Qualifying Disposition Trust
A living trust into which you contribute resource property and land inventory using a tax-deferred rollover.[202] Legal title may change but not beneficial ownership so that land transfer taxes are avoided. An election can be made not to use the rollover if there are offsetting capital losses, exemptions, or tax credits. At your death, the property passes to the beneficiaries and not to your estate such that probate is avoided; however, income taxes are due by the trust from a deemed disposition at fair market value.[203]

---

[200] *In Re Denley's Trust Deed*, [1969] 1 Ch. 373.

[201] *ITA* ss104(4)(a.4); 107.4(1)(e).

[202] *ITA* ss 104(4)(a)(ii.1)(iii)(iv); 107.4(1)(a), (b), (e), (i); (3); 248(1).

[203] *ITA* s 104(2), (4).

RRSP/RRIF Trust

This testamentary trust is beneficiary of your RRSP or RRIF, which receives the proceeds after your death.[204] The trust may deduct from its income any income payments made to beneficiaries.[205]

Resulting Trust

The trust is created by the courts where a property interest Is involved and one and/or others have contributed to it. The "Certainty of Intention" is implied from your conduct[206] based on:

- the old legal adage that the law assumes bargains and not gifts, or

- the prevention of unjust enrichment of one person at the expense of another.[207]

The onus is on the holder of property to show that the property was a gift and not received in trust for another person.[208] Corroboratory evidence may be required if you are deceased.

There is a legal "Presumption of Resulting Trust" where a trust (and not a gift) is presumed to exist when there is:

- a gratuitous transfer of property (eg. bank account),

---

[204]   *ITA* ss146(4), 146.3(3), 149(1)(r), (x).

[205]   *ITA* ss104(6)(a.2), 108(1), 122, 146(4)(c).

[206]   *Goodfriend v Goodfriend*, 1971 CanLII 28 (SCC);
Wawrzyniak v Jagiellicz (1988), 51 DLR(4th) 639 (OCA). *Andrade v Andrade*, 2016 CanLII 368 (ONCA).

[207]   *Pecore v Pecore*, 2007 CanLII 17 (SCC).

[208]   *Johnstone v Johnstone* (1913), 12 DLR 537 (OCA).

- a purchase in the name of yourself and a third person or the third person alone, especially if that person is a non-contributor[209], or

- a failure of purposes in a trust such that the property can revert to you.

The presumption can be rebutted by establishing that a gift was intended either by:

- evidence,[210] or

- the "Presumption of Advancement" in the case of a gratuitous transfer between spouses,[211] or from a parent to a minor child,[212] but not in the case of a parent to an adult child,[213] because the latter often has a role in managing the parents' assets.

You should be clear about your intention regarding joint ownership and beneficiary designations on contracts such as life insurance, registered products, and a joint bank account, because any doubts

---

[209]   *Mroz v Mroz*, 2015 CanLII 171 (ONCA); Bergen v Bergen, 2013 CanLII 492 (BCCA).

[210]   *Re Finlayson Estate*, 2008 CanLII 120 (NSSC).

[211]   BC, MB; ON only for joint tenancy between spouses per *Family Law Act*, RSO 1990, c F.3, s14.

[212]   *Rathwell v Rathwell*, 1978 CanLII 3 (SCC); *Pecore v Pecore*, 2007 CanLII 17 (SCC).

[213]   *Pecore v Pecore*, ibid.; *Madsen Estate v Saylor*, 2007 CanLII 18 (SCC); *McDonald v Eckert*, 2004 CanLII 323 (BCSC).

could cause the beneficiary to be holding the property on resulting trust for your estate.[214]

Secret Trust

If you don't want anyone to know about your provision for another person, then your choice will be a secret trust that only you and your trustee know about.[215] Choose your trustee wisely to ensure that he doesn't keep the property for himself after your death.

Self-Benefit Trust

This is basically an alter ego trust in which you don't have to be age 65 or older. The characteristics are similar:[216]

- only you can have access to the trust income and capital,

- a transfer of property into the trust occurs on a tax-deferred rollover basis,

- the trust survives your death, passes to the named beneficiaries and not to your estate such that probate is avoided,

- income taxes are due at your death by the trust from a deemed disposition at fair market value,[217]

---

[214]   *Neufeld v Neufeld,* 2004 CanLII 25 (BCSC);
         Beaverstock v Beaverstock, 2011 CanLII 413 (BCCA);
         Kerr v Baranow, 2011 CanLII 10 (SCC).

[215]   *Jankowski v Pelek Estate* (1995), 131 DLR(4th) 717 (Man. CA);
         Ferguson Estate v MacLean, 2001 CanLII 154 (NSSC).

[216]   *ITA* s 73(1.02)(b)(ii).

[217]   *ITA* ss 104(4);although new 104(13.4) Implies the
         estate now pays; 107(1)(a), (2)(b); 107.4(4).

- the 21-year deemed disposition rule does not apply until your death,[218] and

- the trust has the same advantages and disadvantages as an alter ego trust.

Spendthrift Trust

When you have someone who spends money recklessly and probably needs protection from creditors, you use a spendthrift trust in which a trustee has discretion in the distribution of income and capital to the beneficiary who, in turn, has no control over the trust and cannot demand a payment. Care must be taken in drafting the trust so that, upon bankruptcy of the beneficiary, the trustee can avoid the federal bankruptcy law, which otherwise would include the trust in the bankrupt's property.[219]

Spousal Trust

As the name implies, this is a trust to provide for your spouse or partner and can be created by court order under dependant's relief laws.[220] It is sometimes referred to as a "qualified spousal trust, post-1971 spousal trust, or a post-1971 partner trust." This trust is used to provide:

- a lifetime income,

- income-splitting between the trust and spouse, but the attribution rules are a problem for a living trust,[221]

- your continued control of assets, and

---

[218]   *ITA* ss104(4)(a.4), 108(1) "trust" (g)(i).

[219]   RSC 1985, c. B-3, s. 7(1).

[220]   *ITA* ss 70(6)(b); 73(1.01)(c)(i), 104(4)(a), 248(9.1).; IT-209R & 209RSR.

[221]   *ITA* ss 74.1-74.5, 104(13.1); IT-511R.

- protection of inheritance (capital) for children in case the spouse/partner remarries after your death.

From an income tax standpoint, the trust can be living or testamentary but a living trust is not advantageous for income purposes because trust income will be attributed back to you. Both you and the trust must be Canadian residents. You contribute property to the trust using a tax-deferred rollover of assets at your cost base.[222] At your death, your spouse (and possibly your partner) can choose to avoid the trust and elect an equalization payment under the family law legislation (see chapter 12).[223] A later separation, divorce, or annulment does not affect the rollover.[224] An encroachment on capital by the spouse/partner is distributed at cost.[225] The principal residence exemption applies.[226] A spousal trust is the only trust that can claim the capital gains exemptions for a qualified small business, farming, or fishing.[227]

Only the spouse can receive all of the income and capital and any income not used is added to capital so that no income is accumulated in the trust.[228] A trust will fail and is said to be "tainted" if income or capital is:[229]

- paid elsewhere than to the spouse/partner, unless:

---

[222] *ITA* ss 70(6)(7); 73(1.01).

[223] *ITA* s.70(6.2).

[224] IT-325R2, para. 13.

[225] *ITA* s107(2).

[226] *ITA* s 40(4).

[227] *ITA* s 110.6(12).

[228] *ITA* ss 70(6); 73(1), (1.01); 75.1; 104(4);
Peardon v MNR (1986), 40 DTC 1045 (TCC).

[229] IT-305R4.

- for the benefit of the spouse/partner,

- under court-ordered dependant's relief, or

- to pay taxes,[230]

- loaned to anyone at non-commercial rates,[231]

- paid for life insurance on the spouse/partner (because at death, other beneficiaries would benefit from the capital),

- cutoff by a remarriage clause, or

- paid at the discretion of the trustee.

The "taint" can be rectified in several ways:[232]

- a reduction of the rollover by the amount of the taint, but the property so used is deemed disposed at fair market value,

- a court order for dependants' relief or to remove clauses inadvertently included in the will (rectification),

- an election to pay testamentary debts, or

- a disclaimer by a beneficiary.

An alternative, if income and/or capital are to be shared, is to create two spousal trusts in your will. One trust is "tainted" but the capital gain on transfer of property to the trust is offset by capital losses, an exemption, or a tax credit. The second trust is untainted and it receives the balance of property by the spousal rollover.

---

[230] *ITA* s 108(4).

[231] IT-305R4 para 16.

[232] *ITA* ss 70(6.2), (7), (8)(c); 73(1); 248(8), (9), (9.1); IT-305R4;
Balaz v Balaz, 2009 CanLII 17973 (OSC);
Gilbert Estate v MNR (1983), 37 DTC 645 (TRB);
Cossitt v MNR, [1949] 4 DTC 617 (Exchequer Ct.) Hillis v R (1983)
CTC 348 (FCA).

The 21-year deemed disposition rule does not apply until the death of the spouse/partner when the trust assets are deemed disposed at fair market value, subject to the capital gains exemptions.[233]

Successive Trust

When you intend your property to be used by successive generations, you would use a successive trust. All of the trusts are considered to be testamentary if their terms are set out in your will.[234]

Trust for a Minor

When you want to provide for a minor without risking attribution of income payments back to you, then set up a trust to hold property until the minor reaches the age of majority, with income payments going to a parent or guardian:[235] The trustee can make application to the court for authority to make income and/or capital payments to third parties for the minor's maintenance and education.

As with an Age 40 trust, income can be retained in the trust and taxed at the minor's graduated rate of taxation until the age of majority.[236]

---

[233] *ITA* ss 104(4)(a), 104(6);new 104(13.4) implies the estate now pays income tax at decease rather than the trust; 107(2), (4.1)(c); 108(1) "trust" (g)(i); 110.6(12).

[234] *ITA* ss 104(1), 108(1) "trust".

[235] eg. *Trustee Act,* RSO 1990, c T.23, ss 36(4)(6); *Children's Law Reform Act,* RSO 1990, c C.12, s 51(1.1).

[236] *ITA* s104(18).

PART C

ESTATE PLANNING GOALS &
TOOLS TO ACHIEVE THEM

CHAPTER 11
LOOKING AFTER YOURSELF

11.1 Safeguarding your health?

11.2 Dealing with your assets?

11.3 What about income?

11.4 Paying bills

11.5 And the funeral etc.

11.1 SAFEGUARDING YOUR HEALTH?

You should create a power of attorney for health or personal care to handle any health issues in case you become incapacitated.

Some of the insurance products should also be considered:

- disability insurance if you can't work for a while,

- critical illness insurance if a stroke, heart attack, or cancer requires lifestyle changes In your house, and

- long term care insurance if you are invalided at home or at a nursing home.

If your health is deteriorating, then consider an accelerated or impaired annuity, or a trust (alter ego, self-benefit, or protective) if you can find a trustworthy person to act as trustee, perhaps your attorney for personal care.

11.2   DEALING WITH YOUR ASSETS?

You should create a power of attorney for property to manage it in case you become incapacitated.

Use life insurance to protect the value of your assets by paying any taxes after your death.

If you don't mind probate and public disclosure, create a will to distribute assets after your death. If you do mind, then keep your assets out of your estate by using will-substitutes, such as gifting, joint ownership, registered products, or trusts.

11.3   WHAT ABOUT INCOME?

1.   Use some of the tax-advantaged vehicles

There are various ways to park money where it can grow tax-free or tax-deferred until used, such as registered products (eg. RRSP, TFSA, RCA) and life insurance. If you have maxed out your RRSP, then purchase universal life insurance.

If you are aged 65+, it may be advantageous to convert some of your RRSP into a RRIF to take advantage of the $2,000 pension income tax credit.

2.   What to do about the house?

Maybe you're sentimental about it, but wasn't that big home supposed to be your retirement nest egg? Remember that you can keep all of the proceeds in a sale with no income tax if it is your principal residence (chapter 18).

Look around for smaller living quarters, such as a condominium to rent or buy or perhaps an apartment. When you've found something suitable, think of selling the house.

If you intend to leave your home to your children, then arrange a **home equity line of credit** (secured by your home) and co-signed by your children who will eventually inherit it.

If you are on a fixed income, house-rich, and cash-poor, then a **reverse mortgage** (chapter 18) provides a lump sum of money until disposition of your house by sale, death or the end of a "fixed term" at which time principal, interest, and title are due.

To increase accessibility to a residence, there are a federal Home Accessibility Tax Credit (HATC) and in Alberta government loans and grants under the Seniors Home Adaptation and Repair Program (SHARP).

3. Segregated Fund + GMWB
The GMWB is a "guaranteed minimum withdrawal balance". Combined with a segregated fund, it provides a guaranteed lifetime income even if the investment reduces to zero, which is unlikely because the fund has capital guarantees at maturity and death. You can name beneficiaries in the contract.

4. RRIF
RRIF withdrawals are taxable income qualifying for the $2,000 pension income tax credit. If withdrawals might increase your income to a level causing a clawback of Old Age Security payments, you might consider the "RRIF Meltdown" strategy (see pp. 48-49), although it is aggressive and should only be used in increasing markets. Talk it over with your financial adviser.

5. Annuity With or Without Life Insurance + Loan
While alive, you can purchase an annuity for income. If you purchase life insurance at the same time, then the annuity provides income and also pays the life insurance premium. The life insurance is then assigned to a financial institution for a loan to be invested to provide income and, additionally, its interest may be tax-deductible.

If your children are beneficiaries of the life insurance, get them to pay the premiums—they will receive the proceeds after the loan is paid off at your death.

6. What if you don't have a pension plan

If you are a business-owner, key-executive of a business, or are self-employed, arrange for an **IPP** if your annual income is $100,000+ and the business is incorporated. Contributions to an IPP are tax-deductible to the business and can also be used to offset profits from the sale of your business. At retirement, you can withdraw monthly income from your IPP or transfer it to a LIF or LRIF, or purchase an annuity that pays monthly Income.

Don't forget the new government plans: a **Pooled Registered Pension Plan** or **Voluntary Retirement Savings Plan**, a **Target Benefit Plan**, and the provincial **Registered Pension Plan**.

7. Support from Children

Interestingly, some legislation, such as section 32 of the Ontario Family Law Act, imposes an obligation on a child to support a parent:

> "Every child who is not a minor has an obligation to provide support, in accordance with need, for his or her parent who has cared for or provided support for the child, to the extent that the child Is capable of doing so."[237]

11.4 PAYING BILLS

1. Joint account

A joint bank account with a trusted Individual is an easy way to pay bills but can have the problems listed in chapter 6. Attach a memorandum that the account is joint only for paying bills.

2. Power of attorney for property

Specify in the power that it is only for paying bills when and if you cannot do so for yourself.

---

[237] RSO 1990, c F.3, s 32.

3. Alter ego trust

Specify that the trustee can use trust monies only to pay bills on your behalf and has no other access to the trust income or capital.

11.5   AND THE FUNERAL ETC.

In Appendix A (pp. 191-193), there are lists of things to consider ahead of your passing. There is also an income tax break for pre-paying an Eligible Funeral Arrangement (EFA) with a funeral home. EFA funding is not tax-deductible, has a limit of $35,000, and It grows tax-free.[238]

---

[238]   ITA s 148.1, IT-531 archived.

CHAPTER 12
SUPPORT FOR SPOUSE/PARTNER

Support raises several questions:

1. Is there an outstanding support order for a spouse/partner?

2. Is there a domestic, marriage, or cohabitation contract between them dealing with property and support?

3. Were the spouse/partners married or cohabiting? The law doesn't necessarily treat them equally and the different treatment of a spouse and an unmarried partner Is not unconstitutional nor contrary to the Charter of Rights and Freedoms.[239] A partner may have to rely on dependants' relief laws and the laws of constructive or resulting trusts or unjust enrichment.[240]

4. Will your spouse choose rights under your will or an equalization claim under family law legislation.[241]

---

[239] *Nova Scotia v Walsh*, 2002 CanLII 83 (SCC).

[240] *Kerr v Baranow*, 2011 CanLII 10 (SCC).

[241] Provinces where:
-a spouse chooses a claim under the will or an equalization: ON, NU, NT
-a spouse can claim both: MB, NL, NS, QC, SK, AB, NB
-an unmarried partner can claim under the will or an equalization: NU, NT
-an unmarried partner can claim both: MB, NS, QC, SK.
Provinces without choice: BC, PE, YT.

12.1 The equalization claim

12.2 Support by income payments

12.3 Support by transfers of capital

12.1 THE EQUALIZATION CLAIM

After your death and assuming that you provided support for your spouse/partner in your will, she can choose to claim either under your will or to make a family law equalization claim. A claim must be made in a fixed period of time after death (eg. 6 months).

An equalization calculates the "net family property" of the spouses by dividing the total of

- the value of assets acquired by both spouses during marriage,

- the increase in value of their property brought into the marriage,

- to the exclusion of:

    - pre-marriage assets (except the matrimonial home),

    - debts and liabilities,

    - gifts and inheritance from a third person,

    - damages of a personal nature (eg. injury),

    - life insurance proceeds[242], and

    - assets excluded by domestic agreement.

If the net family property of the deceased exceeds that of the survivor, then the survivor is entitled to ½ the difference. The equalization payment can be made as a lump sum or by installments and a spousal rollover can be used. In order to satisfy an equalization payment, the estate may have to reduce, sell or eliminate other

---

[242] eg. *FLA* s 6(6); *Grant v Grant*, 2010 CanLII 553 (ABQB).

beneficiaries' gifts, including life insurance proceeds. Tax liability for the estate may be incurred.[243]

The effect of a claim is that the spouse/partner loses rights in the will (eg. to act as executor), gifts in the will, and rights to a trust (eg. spousal trust).[244]

The disruption caused by an equalization claim can be avoided by:

- a domestic, marriage or cohabitation contract in which the right to claim is waived or certain assets are stipulated to be used for any claim,

- a will drafted to match or exceed an equalization claim, possibly with an instruction to use certain assets first,

- a Joint Partner Trust that contains all of the family assets, or

- leaving assets, life insurance, pension, and registered products to your spouse in an amount exceeding the equivalent to a claim.

12.2 SUPPORT BY INCOME PAYMENTS

1. Family business

If you have a family business, hire your spouse/partner to be paid compensation reasonably related to the work performed.

2. Pensions & Pension Income Splitting

If you contributed to CPP/QPP, then upon your decease, payments are made to a spouse/partner of a death benefit up to $2,500 and a survivor income benefit.

---

[243] *Matthews v Matthews,* 2012 CanLII 933 (ONSC).

[244] *Anderson v Anderson Estate,* 1990 CanLII 6676 (OSC);
Reid v Reid (1999), 35 ETR(2d) 267 (OSC Div)).

CPP and QPP income can be split once both you and your spouse/ partner qualify for the retirement benefits.

You can lower your total family income tax by sharing up to 50% of your pension income with your spouse/partner on the assumption that the latter is in a lower tax bracket.

Other taxable income payments from the following can also be split:

- at any age:

  - from a RPP or IPP,

  - from an annuity purchased with LIF funds or

  - from a RRIF, LIF, LRIF, PRIF, DPSP In the event of your death

- at age 65+:

  - from a RRIF, LIF, LRIF, PRIF, DPSP,

  - from an annuity purchased with RRSP funds, or

  - from a GIC of an insurance company where interest is reported as annuity income.

Don't forget the $2,000 pension income tax credit.

The Family Tax Cut (up to $2,000 income split) introduced in 2014 is now replaced by the Canada Child Benefit.

3. Spousal RRSP

This is another way to split income. You can open a RRSP in the name of and owned by your spouse/partner until her age 71 with tax-deductible contributions from you. When you die, a final contribution can be made to a spousal RRSP within 60 days of the end of the year of death as long as you have contribution room.[245] When the spouse/

---

[245] *ITA* s 146(5.1).

partner turns 71, the RRSP can be withdrawn as taxable income, rolled tax-deferred into a RRIF, or used to purchase an annuity. The RRIF and annuity provide periodic income.

The RRSP can act as a source of emergency funds but withdrawals within 3 years of contribution may be attributed back to your income.

4. Your TFSA

Make your spouse/partner the successor account holder and beneficiary of your TFSA so that, at your death, the spouse/partner can continue to receive the payments.[246] If simply named as the sole beneficiary, a spouse/partner can apply to assume ownership of the TFSA, continue the contract, and change the payments and beneficiaries.

5. Your RRSP

You can use your RRSP to provide support but you have to determine whether your RRSP is unmatured (not yet making retirement payments) or matured (making payments).[247] For a matured RRSP, name your spouse/partner as successor annuitant and sole beneficiary of the RRSP who continues to receive the RRSP payments as taxable income. Probate is avoided. Alternatively, if simply named as the sole beneficiary, a spouse/partner can apply to assume ownership of the RRSP, continue the contract, and change the payments and beneficiaries.

6. Your RRIF, LIF, RPP

You can avoid probate and defer income tax (not taxed in your estate) by naming your spouse/partner as successor annuitant and beneficiary of your RRIF or LIF who becomes the annuitant and owner and

---

[246]   *ITA* s 146.2; CRA Guide RC4477 & *Death of a TFSA Holder*.

[247]   *ITA* ss 60(1), 146(1), (8.8), (8.91); IT-500R; CRA pamphlet RC4177.

can continue to receive the income payments as taxable income plus change the payments and beneficiaries.[248]

Similarly for your RPP, name your spouse/partner as beneficiary in which case, when you die, the periodic payments can continue if your RPP is federal or located in some provinces or you've chosen a joint and last survivor guarantee.[249]

7. Segregated fund

Name your spouse/partner to receive the proceeds periodically after your death. Income tax may be due on capital gains.

8. Your IPP

At your decease:

- if your spouse/partner is named as beneficiary, she can:

    - continue to receive any pension payments at the full amount if there is a guarantee period and otherwise with a 1/3 reduction, or

    - use a rollover to transfer lump-sum proceeds to her own RRSP or RRIF with sufficient room, and

- any remaining surplus in the IPP is paid to your estate where it will be distributed to beneficiaries of your will and taxable to them.

9. Life Insurance

You purchase:

---

[248]   *ITA* ss 60(1), 146(8.2), 146.3(1); CRA pamphlet RC4178.

[249]   *ITA* ss 60(1), 60.02, 147.3(7); AB, BC, MB, SK; see provincial Pension Benefit Acts.

- a joint first-to-die policy with you and your spouse/partner as the lives insured and your spouse/partner as beneficiary or

- a policy on yourself and transfer it tax-free to your spouse/partner.[250]

While you are alive, your spouse/partner can create income either by taking a loan directly from the insurance company or by assigning the policy to a financial institution for a loan. At your death, the insurance proceeds, less the loan amount, can be paid as tax-free periodic payments to your spouse/partner to be invested for income.

10. Joint Survivor Life Annuity
You purchase this annuity from an insurance company to provide lifetime income for you and your spouse/partner.

11. Spousal Trust
Keep in mind that a trust does require setup and maintenance costs. A spousal trust for income is created in your will with the spouse as the only person who can receive the trust income; otherwise, the trust is "tainted." If income is to be shared, then create two spousal trusts in your will, one tainted and the other not.

12. Joint Partner Trust
A living trust in which you and your spouse/partner are the beneficiaries and have sole access to the income. When you die, the trust continues to provide lifetime income to your spouse/partner.

13. Life insurance trust
You could purchase life insurance and set up a trust inside or outside your will to receive the proceeds when you die. After the trust receives the money, it can provide income for your spouse/partner whose lower rate of income tax can be used.

---

[250]   *ITA* s 148(8.1).

14. Income Splitting using RESP

If a RESP has you and your spouse/partner as joint subscribers but only you as a contributor, then if the plan collapses at your death, contributions are withdrawn tax-free and earnings can go to the non-contributor's RRSP or spousal RRSP if sufficient contribution room exists.

15. Pension Income Credit

Qualifying pension income paid to your spouse/partner upon your decease can receive the pension income tax credit.

12.3 SUPPORT BY TRANSFERS OF CAPITAL

1. Your Will

You can make your spouse/partner a capital beneficiary in your will. Give your executor some discretion in your will to consider receipts to be capital or income if there are different income and capital beneficiaries.

Be careful if naming your spouse/partner in your will as a beneficiary of a contract because a designation in your will overrides any earlier designation in a contract (eg. RRSP, RRIF, life insurance).

2. Gifting & Spousal Rollover

You can gift property to your spouse/partner while you are alive. A transfer of property is a taxable event unless the asset is non-appreciating or appreciating with offsetting losses, exemptions, or tax credits. Watch out for income produced by the property because the income might be attributed back to you but not secondary Income earned on the attributed income.[251] You can also gift property on your deathbed or in your will without attribution problems.

You can give property to your spouse/partner by using a tax-deferred spousal rollover to transfer capital property so that the recognition

---

[251] *ITA* ss 74.1-75.

of taxable capital gains is deferred until the spouse/partner disposes of the property or at her death.[252] You and your spouse/partner must be Canadian residents. A transfer does not have to be all of your property but can be property-by-property. An election can be made not to rollover the property but to incur the taxes if there are offsetting losses, exemptions, and credits.[253] As the recognition of capital gains is deferred, the ultimate tax liability can be offset by purchasing joint last-to-die life insurance, payable on the death of the spouse/partner.

3. Loan and/or TFSA for spouse/partner

You can make a loan to your spouse/partner at the ITA prescribed rate. For such a loan, there will be no attribution back to you of the loan, its income earned, nor its forgiveness in your will.[254]

You could loan money to your spouse/partner to start a TFSA and there should be no attribution back to you of the loan or of resulting income and capital gains.

4. Joint tenancy

You could share an asset with your spouse/partner through a joint tenancy with right of survivorship. The asset can provide support for either or both of you during your lifetimes and, at your death, your spouse/partner automatically receives full ownership. Income tax is due when the joint tenancy is created but could be offset by losses, exemptions, tax credits or delayed using the spousal rollover.

---

[252] *ITA* ss 70(6), (6.2), (7), 70(7),(12), (13); 73; IT-305R4.

[253] *ITA* s 70(6.2).

[254] *ITA* s 80(2)(a), Regu. 4301.

5. Your TFSA

There are two ways that you can use your TFSA.[255] One way is to name your spouse/partner as beneficiary to receive your TFSA's pre-death income and capital gains tax-free.

Another way is to make your spouse/partner the successor account holder and beneficiary of your TFSA so that, at your decease, she can transfer the proceeds to her TFSA without affecting her contribution room.

If simply named as the sole beneficiary, a spouse/partner can apply to assume ownership of the TFSA, continue the contract, and change the payments and beneficiaries.

6. Your RRSP

If your RRSP is unmatured (not yet making payments),[256] name your spouse/partner as sole beneficiary who can transfer the proceeds at your death to her own RRSP, RRIF, PRPP, or purchase an annuity. Contribution room is not required. The proceeds are known as a "refund of premiums." Your estate avoids probate and income tax is deferred (not taxed in your estate).

7. Your RRIF

You can avoid probate and defer income tax (not taxed in your estate) by naming your spouse/partner as beneficiary who transfers the proceeds at your death to her own RRSP, RRIF, PRPP, or purchases an annuity.[257]

---

[255] *ITA* s 146.2; CRA Guide RC4477 & *Death of a TFSA Holder*.

[256] *ITA* ss 60(1); 146(1),(8.9); 146.3(2)(f); IT-500R; CRA pamphlet RC4177; Tax Guide T4040 ch. 6

[257] *ITA* ss 60(1), 146(8.2), 146.3(1); CRA pamphlet RC4178; Tax Guide T4040 ch 6

8. Your RPP

Probate can be avoided and income tax deferred (not taxed in your estate) by naming your spouse/partner as beneficiary and, when you die, the proceeds can be paid as a lump sum (not periodic payments) that can be transferred into her own RPP, RRSP, or RRIF. [258]

9. Your PRPP

You can avoid probate and income tax deferred (not taxed in your estate) by naming your spouse/partner as "successor member" who acquires your rights under the plan. Alternatively, you can name your spouse/partner as beneficiary who can transfer the proceeds to her own PRPP, RPP, RRSP, RRIF, or acquire an annuity. [259]

10. Your DPSP

Name your spouse/partner as beneficiary who can transfer the proceeds at your death to her own RRSP, RRIF, DPSP, RPP, or PRPP.

11. Segregated investment fund

You could invest in a segregated fund and name your spouse/partner as beneficiary so that when you die proceeds are paid to your spouse/partner outside the estate without probate; however, income tax is due on any capital gains. For a tax-free continuation of a non-registered contract, name your spouse/partner as successor owner and successor annuitant.

12. Life Insurance

You purchase:

- a joint first-to-die policy with you and your spouse/partner as the lives insured and your spouse/partner as beneficiary or

---

[258]   *ITA* ss 60(1), 147.3(7); see provincial Pension Benefits Acts.

[259]   *ITA* ss147.5(21) & 60(l), Tax Guide T4040 ch 6.

- a universal life policy on yourself, overfund it to create a large death benefit, then transfer it tax-free to your spouse/partner.[260]

At your death, the proceeds are payable tax-free to your spouse/partner as a lump sum.

13. Spousal Trust

Property can be transferred to the trust by a tax-deferred spousal rollover. Only the spouse can use the trust capital; otherwise, the trust will be "tainted." If capital is to be shared, then create two spousal trusts in your will, one tainted and the other not. Because the recognition of capital gains is deferred, the ultimate tax liability can be offset by purchasing joint last-to-die life insurance, payable on the death of the spouse/partner.

14. Joint Partner Trust

A living trust in which you and your spouse/partner are the beneficiaries and have sole access to the capital. The trust survives your decease and continues to be available as capital to your spouse/partner.

---

[260] *ITA* s 148(8.1).

CHAPTER 13
SUPPORT FOR CHILDREN

As stated in chapter 2.3, the term "children" can include those born in or out of wedlock, adopted, stepchildren, and children born before or after a designation as a beneficiary.[261] The age of majority for a child is 18 in some provinces and 19 in others.[262] There is no general obligation on a parent to support an adult child, except in divorce proceedings or full time education.[263]

If the child is a minor, there are various types of persons who can oversee and act for the child:

- a **guardian** (Quebec:"tutor") protects the child and its property,

- a **custodian** controls the child's assets, and

---

[261]   eg. Ontario *Children's Law Reform Act,* RSO 1990, c C.12, s 1(1); *Brule v Brule,* [1979] 2 SCR 343.

[262]   Age 18: AB, SK, MB, ON, QC, PE; Age 19 in others.

[263]   *Harrington v Harrington,* 1981 CanLII 1762 (OCA); *Divorce Act,* RSC 1985, c 3(2nd Supp.), s 2(1)(b). *Family Law Act,* RSO 1990, c F.3, s 31(1).

- a **trustee** acts in the best interest of the child. The trust terms are flexible to avoid the restrictions on a guardian and custodian.

Before distributing assets, it would be wise to await the appointment of one of the above because a minor cannot sign a release.

Some provincial governments have an Office of the Children's Lawyer to represent minors and unborn persons in estate and trust cases but not to administer an estate nor to act as guardian.

13.1 Support by income payments

13.2 Support by transfers of capital

13.1 SUPPORT BY INCOME PAYMENTS

1. Government pensions
If you contributed to CPP/QPP, then upon your decease, payments of a survivor's monthly income benefit can be made to unmarried dependent children attending school full-time.

2. Family business, Child's RRSP
You can hire your child for pay reasonably related to work performed. If pay involves shares in the business, the attribution rules may apply to dividend income paid to a minor ("kiddie tax").

Again using a family business, you can hire your child who can use the earned income to create a RRSP. Your child can open an account at any age, even as a minor with your letter of consent as parent and the child as annuitant.

3. Segregated Fund
Name your (grand)child as beneficiary to receive the proceeds periodically after your death. Income tax may be due on capital gains.

4. Life Insurance

You purchase life insurance on yourself and name the child as beneficiary. At your death, the insurance company can be instructed to pay the tax-free proceeds periodically to the child and not by lump sum, in either case to a parent or guardian if a minor.

Additionally, ownership of the policy can be transferred tax-free to the child at Its age of majority.[264] The child can then create income either by taking a loan directly from the insurance company or by assigning the policy to a financial institution for a loan.

5. Trusts in general

There are various trusts that can be used but remember that they require setup and ongoing maintenance costs. The use of the trust is based on the child receiving income payments from the trustee. The child's lower rate of income tax can be used without funds actually being transferred if the amount is considered "payable" or "paid," such as to a private school for a minor. A trust for a minor is usually in your will and not a living trust because the income tax attribution rules will otherwise attribute trust income back to you until the minor achieves majority.[265] Upon majority, the attribution rules no longer apply.

6. Life Insurance Trust

You purchase life insurance on yourself, set up the trust as beneficiary in your will, and name the child as trust beneficiary. At your decease, the trust is funded with the life insurance proceeds to provide income payments. The trust is particularly useful for a minor who is unable to provide a receipt for the insurance proceeds and unable to provide consent if designated Irrevocably.

---

[264] *ITA* ss148(8), (8.2).

[265] *ITA* ss 74.1(2), 74.3.

7.   Family Trust

You name as trust beneficiaries the family members, such as your spouse/partner plus children (of one or more marriages) or simply the children alone. The assets transferred into the trust are taxable and not tax-deferred. Income-splitting is possible as trust income is distributed to the spouse/partner and children assuming they have a tax rate lower than the trust.

8.   Age 40 Trust

A trust in which the child is beneficiary of the trust which retains income until payout at a pre-determined age.

9.   Secret Trust

This trust is useful to provide for children out of wedlock, known only to you and your trustee.

13.2 SUPPORT BY TRANSFERS OF CAPITAL

1.   Your Will

You can make your child a capital beneficiary in your will. Give your executor some discretion in your will to consider receipts to be capital or income if there are different income and capital beneficiaries.

Be careful if naming your minor child as irrevocable beneficiary of a contract or in your will because a minor cannot provide consent to changes. And remember that a designation in your will overrides an earlier designation In a contract.

2.   Gifting

You can always give cash to your child but a transfer of capital property to your child may be a taxable event presently for you unless there are offsetting losses, exemptions, or tax credits. If the child is a minor, capital gains will not be attributed back to you,[266] as is also the case with secondary income earned on attributed income.

If the gift is to be delayed until a specified age, use a "gift over" so that if the child dies, then the gift doesn't fail but passes to the child's own children or to another child. Your lawyer will understand this.

3. Loan and/or TFSA for child

You can make a loan to your child at the ITA prescribed rate. For such a loan, there will be no attribution back to you of the loan, its income earned, nor its forgiveness in your will.[267]

You could loan money to your child who has attained the age of majority to start a TFSA and there should be no attribution back to you of resulting income and capital gains.

4. Joint tenancy

You could share an asset with your child through a joint tenancy with right of survivorship but be clear in your intentions. At your death, your child automatically receives full ownership if you intended a gift. If you intended simply to have the child managing your affairs and paying bills, then the child probably will be found to be holding the asset on a resulting trust for your estate. Any income tax is due when the joint tenancy is created but that would not be the case for cash nor if an asset has offsetting losses, exemptions, or tax credits.

5. Your TFSA

You can name your child as beneficiary to receive tax-free at your death your pre-death income and capital gains.[268]

---

[266] *ITA* ss 74.1-75.

[267] *ITA* s 80(2)(a), Regu 4301.

[268] *ITA* s146.2; CRA Guide RC4477 & *Death of a TFSA Holder.*

6. Your RRSP/RRIF

If your (grand)child is financially dependent on you, name him as beneficiary. At your death, he can transfer the proceeds to his own RRSP, RRIF or, if a minor, purchase an annuity to age 18.[269] The proceeds are known as a "refund of premiums." Probate is thereby avoided and income tax is deferred (not taxed in your estate).

7. Life insurance

You purchase universal life insurance on your (grand)child, overfund the policy to create a large death benefit and, at the child's age of majority, transfer ownership of the policy tax-free to the child. The child then has her own life insurance and a capital base against which to borrow or to use as collateral for a loan.

8. Cascading Life Insurance

You have excess funds that you wish to pass to successive generations. You purchase universal life insurance on the life of your child, overfund it with the excess monies, name your child as contingent owner and your grandchild as beneficiary. At your decease, your child assumes ownership of the policy and names the grandchild as the new contingent owner. The process repeats at the death of your child. The capital passes tax-free at each stage from owner to owner and can provide income either as a capital base against which to borrow or be used as collateral for a loan.

9. Your RPP, PRPP

You name your financially-dependent (grand)child as beneficiary who, at your death, can rollover the RPP proceeds as a lump sum (not periodic payments) to her own RPP, RRSP, RRIF, PRPP, or

---

[269]   *ITA* ss 60(l)(v)(B.01); 60.02; 146(1), (1.1), (8.8), (8.9); 146.3; IT-500R; CRA pamphlets RC4177, 4178; Tax Guide T4040 ch 6.

purchase an annuity.[270] Probate is avoided and income tax is deferred (not taxed in your estate). The same applies to a PRPP.[271]

10. Name irrevocable beneficiaries; restrict capital

Where you intend to have a new spouse/partner for whom a lifetime income will be provided (eg. spousal trust) but you also want to pre-serve capital for children of a former marriage, then name the children as irrevocable beneficiaries and restrict the spouse's access to capital. Changes cannot be made in the contract by your new spouse/partner without the consent of the children or their guardian (if a minor). Do not name a minor as irrevocable beneficiary because a minor cannot provide consent.

11. Trust for Minor or Informal Trust (ITF)

The trust can be used to split capital with a minor because the attribution rules do not attribute capital back to you.

13. Asset Protection Trust

If you intend to marry again but have valuable property to be pre-served for your other family, then transfer the property to this trust with an instruction to the trustee on when and how to deal with the property. The transfer is a taxable event but possibly there are off-setting exemptions, such as the principal residence exemption, or losses or tax credits.

14. Successive Trusts

If you intend property to be of use to successive generations, then you transfer it to a succession of trusts, living or in your will.[272]

---

[270] *ITA* ss 60(1), 60.02, 147.3(7); Tax Guide T4040 ch 6.

[271] *ITA* ss 147.5 & 60(l), Tax Guide T4040 Ch 6.

[272] *ITA* ss 104(1), 108(1) "trust."

CHAPTER 14
SUPPORT FOR THE DISABLED

You should be careful when arranging support for a disabled person who is financially dependent on you because provincial disability benefits may be reduced or cut off if income and assets exceed certain limits. A parent's legal obligation to support a disabled child, even if an adult, can arise in divorce proceedings for the necessities of life.

The persons appointed to represent and manage the affairs of a disabled person are:

- a trustee,

- a guardian (Quebec: "curator" or "tutor"),

- an attorney under a power of attorney (Quebec: "mandatary" under a "mandate") who can act in place of the disabled person for anything except creating or changing a will, or

- an executor (Quebec: "liquidator") if a disabled person had at one time sufficient mental capacity to make a will, hopefully naming beneficiaries to prevent an intestacy.

Before distributing an estate, it would be wise to await the appointment of one of these persons in order to obtain a release from liability.

14.1　Support by income payments

14.2　Support by transfers of capital

14.1　SUPPORT BY INCOME PAYMENTS

1.　RDSP Withdrawals

Contributions, which are not tax-deductible, can be made by anyone to a RDSP. Federal monies in the form of a grant and bond are available. Generally, a plan is exempted from the calculation of provincial disability benefits.

Lifetime Disability Assistance Payments (LDAP) are composed of non-taxable contributions and a taxable portion (growth, government grants and bonds, rollover amounts). A repayment of part or all of a grant or bond may be required.

2.　Life Insurance

You purchase life insurance on yourself and name the disabled person as beneficiary of the policy to receive the insurance proceeds as periodic payments tax-free upon your death.

Life insurance on the disabled person is more difficult to obtain but possible in a smaller amount with relaxed underwriting.

3.　TFSA for Disabled Person

If a disabled person has sufficient mental capacity, start a TFSA for him in which he can shelter future growth of contributions tax-free, make withdrawals tax-free, and the withdrawals will not be included in his income nor affect income-tested government benefits.

4.　Accelerated Annuity or Impaired Annuity

These are annuities with higher early payments where an annuitant suffers from a life-threatening illness, has a shortened life expectancy, and wants to cover the costs of care.

5. Income Tax Credits & Deductions

The Income Tax Act has various credits and deductions to assist the disabled person, the caregiver, and the family, all of which are detailed in CRA Guide RC4064 "Medical and Disability-Related Information" and the new Income Tax Folios S1-F1-C1, C2, C3. C1 deals with the Medical Expense Tax Credit, C2 with the Disability Tax Credit, and C3 with the Disability Supports Deduction, all of which in September 2014 replaced IT-519R2 "Medical Expense and Disability Tax Credits and Attendant Care Expense Deduction." The new Canada Caregiver Credit (CCC) provides a tax credit for the caregiver of infirm dependants.

6. Trusts in general

There are various trusts that can be used but remember that they require setup and ongoing maintenance costs that may deter their use. In order not to affect government disability payments, the trusts must be discretionary so that the disabled person as beneficiary has no right to demand trust money and no control over the trust. Additionally, name a trust beneficiary to receive the income after the 21-year period of maximum accumulation of income so that It does not affect the disabled person's government benefits.

7. Henson Trust

This is a well-recognized trust used in the disabled situation without limit on the property contributed.[273] It can be living or testamentary in your will.

8. Lifetime Benefit Trust

A testamentary trust resembling a Henson trust set up to support solely a mentally infirm person, whether a spouse/partner or dependent (grand)child.[274]

---

[273] *Ontario v Henson* (1988), 28 ETR 121 (OSC Div); (1989), 36 ETR 192 (OCA); *ITA* ss 60.01, 60.011, 104(14), IT-394R2.

[274] *ITA* s 60.011(1).

9. Disability Trust, Qualified Disability Trust

A Disability trust is set up outside your will with provincial approval and monitoring, with trust value not exceeding $100,000.

A Qualified Disability Trust is testamentary designed to pay income to a disabled person who must qualify for the Disability Tax Credit.[275]

10. Life Insurance Trust

A testamentary trust set up to receive and invest the proceeds from life insurance on you in order to make periodic income payments after your death. The trust is useful if the disabled person is unable to manage their affairs. It also avoids creditor claims against your estate.

11. Secret Trust

A trust known only to yourself and the trustee. Risky, because if you are found out, then provincial disability payments may be affected.

14.2 SUPPORT BY TRANSFERS OF CAPITAL

1. RDSP

At decease, the plan proceeds pass to the disabled person's estate and are subject to probate.[276] Contributions are not taxable but growth is taxable as income. Government grants over the past 10 years are to be repaid but, while alive, the beneficiary can arrange for those amounts to be reduced by obtaining a medical certificate certifying his or her life expectancy to be 5 years or less.

2. Your RRSP, RRIF, RPP, PRPP

You name as beneficiary of your RRSP or RRIF your (grand)child who is financially-dependent on you owing to physical or mental

---

[275] *ITA* s122(1)-(3).

[276] *ITA* ss 60.02, 146, 146.4(4)(p).

impairment. At your death the proceeds, called "refund of premiums," may be transferred to her own RRSP, RRIF, RDSP, or if a minor, an annuity to age 18.[277]

You name the disabled person as beneficiary of your RPP or PRPP who, at your death, can then rollover a lump sum amount received (not periodic payments) to her own RPP, RRSP, RRIF, PRPP, or RDSP.[278]

In either case, probate is avoided and income tax is deferred (not taxed in your estate) but the amounts may affect eligibility for benefits.

3. RESP

If the disabled person does not attend post-secondary education and the plan has existed for 10 years, then the investment income earned in the plan can be rolled tax-deferred into the beneficiary's RDSP.[279] Government grants have to be repaid but the contributions are paid out tax-free.

4. Trusts in general

As stated previously, the trust should be discretionary so that the disabled person Is deemed not to have received the trust property, thereby not affecting provincial disability payments. Also, a trust beneficiary should be named to receive the capital after the 21-year period of realization of capital gains so that it does not affect the disabled person's government benefits.

---

[277] *ITA* ss 60(l)(v)(B.01), 146(1), (1.1), (8.8), 146.3; IT-500R; CRA pamphlets RC4177, 4178; Tax Guide T4040 ch 6.

[278] *ITA* ss 60(1), 147.3(7); Tax Guide T4040 ch 6.

[279] *ITA* ss 146.1(1.1), (1.2).

5.   Principal Residence Trust

This is a living or testamentary trust designed to hold title to a principal residence for the disabled person. The value of such benefit is not generally included in the calculation of government benefits.

6.   Asset Protection Trust or Protective Trust

To protect the disabled person from creditors, you create this living or testamentary trust in which the trustee has full discretion in the distribution of capital.

7.   Inheritance Trust

A trust with assets not exceeding $100,000, to hold an inheritance that might otherwise disqualify a person from disability benefits.

CHAPTER 15
COURT-IMPOSED SUPPORT

Court-imposed remedies are based on:

- legislation to prevent a strain on the social welfare system,[280]

- unjust enrichment where the deceased has been enriched at the expense of a dependant without any legal reason for doing so, or

- a moral claim derived from the deceased's expressed intentions by will or memorandum or conduct.[281]

---

[280] AB: *Dependants Relief Act* ,RSA 2000 c D-10.5;

BC: *Wills, Estates and Successions Act*, SBC 2009, c 13;

MB: *Dependants Relief Act*, CCSM c D37;

NB: *Provisions of Dependants Act*, RSNB 1973, c P-22.3;

NL: *Family Relief Act*, RSNL 1990 c F-3;

NS: *Testator's Family Maintenance Act*, RSNS 1989 c 465 &
   Matrimonial Property Act, RSNS 1989 c 275;

ON: *SLRA*, RSO 1990, c S.26;

PE: *Dependants of a Deceased Person Relief Act*, RSPEI 1988 c D-7;

QC: *CCQ* arts 684-695;

SK: *Dependants Relief Act*, SS 1996 c D-25.01,

YT: *Dependants Relief Act*, RSY 2002 c 56.

[281] Moral entitlement is relevant in AB, BC, and ON.

The problem with these remedies is the cost of going to court to prove them.

15.1 Monetary award

15.2 Non-monetary award

15.1 MONETARY AWARD

1. Provincial Support Legislation

Provincial law plays a large part in the relationship of persons and their property and, as a result, estate planning comes into contact with family law when dealing with dependants who look to you for support, such as your spouse/partner, child, parent and sibling. Dependants may require income for their lifetime and capital from time to time, such as to purchase an automobile.

A court is permitted by provincial legislation to order support for a dependant by:

- varying your will,

- using your assets whether inside or outside your estate,

- binding your estate to existing support orders, and

- requiring that life insurance proceeds be brought into your estate for support purposes, in spite of irrevocable beneficiaries.[282]

A court can use the legislation to discourage a forfeiture clause that disinherits someone.[283]

---

[282] *Matthews v Matthews*, 2012 CanLII 933 (ONSC).

[283] *Kent v McKay* (1982) CanLII 788 (BCSC).

Child support has federal and provincial guidelines, to be supplemented by special or extraordinary expenses.[284] Spousal support also has federal guidelines.[285] Payments are generally non-taxable for child support and taxable for spousal support. Security for support obligations can be arranged with life insurance on you with your spouse or children named as irrevocable beneficiaries.

2. Quantum Meruit

An order for monetary compensation, known in law by its latin name, "quantum meruit," (pronounced "kwan-tum mer-oo-it") is made for services rendered, much like a contract.[286] The claim is based on unjust enrichment[287] but there can be difficulties with proof; so, a court will examine:

- intentions of you and the other person,

- services rendered by the other person to you, and

- the non-existence of a justification for the services (eg. contract, gift, or law). [288]

In a family situation, a child might file a claim for services rendered, such as:

- caring for a parent thereby losing a chance for independence or giving up an education or a career,

---

[284] Federal *Child Support Guidelines*, SOR/97-175,
Ontario *Child Support Guidelines*, OReg 391/97.

[285] Federal *Spousal Support Advisory Guidelines*, SOR/97-175;
Fisher v Fisher, 2008 CanLII 11 (ONCA)

[286] *Peter v Beblow*, 1993 CanLII 126 (SCC);
Deglman v Guarantee Trust, 1954 CanLII 2 (SCC).

[287] *Pettkus v Becker*, 1980 CanLII 22 (SCC).

[288] *Garland v Consumers Gas*, 2004 CanLII 25 (SCC).
Granger v Granger, 2016 CanLII 945 ONSC

- providing care which saved the family the costs of caring for a parent, or

- putting labour and money into the alteration of property for a parent.

15.2 NON-MONETARY AWARD

Where a monetary award is inadequate, then a court will entertain another type of remedy.

1. Dependants' Relief Trust

A trust created by the courts based on moral obligations found in provincial legislation so that property is held for the benefit of a dependant.[289] The trust can be a spousal trust to defer taxes.

2. Constructive Trust

Where your estate will be unjustly enriched or where a moral claim can be made by a dependant against your estate, a court can impose a constructive trust on your estate to hold property for the benefit of the dependant. A moral claim can even include non-dependants, such as an ex-wife or adult children.[290]

3. Resulting Trust

Where someone has property of your estate without any legal reason for having it, a court can impose a resulting trust on a holder of the property in favour of support for a dependant.

---

[289] *ITA* s 248(9.1).

[290] *Tataryn v Tataryn Estate*, 1994 CanLII 51 (SCC);
Cummings v Cummings Estate, 2004 CanLII 9339 (OCA);
Perilli v Foley Estate, 2006 CanLII 3285 (OSC).

4. Proprietary Estoppel ("Raising an Equity")

This occurs when a person has been induced unjustly by you or your executor to rely on a right or benefit which is now being withdrawn to the detriment of the person. A court can impose a proprietary estoppel to prevent an unconscionable retraction of the right or benefit.[291]

5. Joint Family Venture

This is a new concept invented by the Supreme Court of Canada (Mr. Justice Cromwell):

> "where wealth is accumulated as a result of joint effort, as evidenced by the nature of the parties' relationship and their dealings with each other, the law of unjust enrichment should reflect that reality."[292]

The remedy is flexible but probably will result in a monetary award and/or a constructive trust. This is particularly useful for an unmarried partner but a better solution for that person would be a domestic agreement at the start of the relationship.

---

[291] *Cowderoy v Sorkos Estate*, 2012 CanLII 1921 (ONSC);
Spadafora v Gabriele, 2011 CanLII 6686 (ONSC);
Schwark v Cutting, 2010 CanLII 61 (ONCA);
Eberts v Carleton Condominium, 2000 CanLII 16889 (OCA);
Sabey v Beardsley, 2013 CanLII 642 (BCSC).

[292] *Kerr v Baranow*, 2011 CanLII 10 (SCC) para. 85.

CHAPTER 16
SUPPORT FOR PETS

You may be concerned for the welfare of your pet after your decease, which may not seem important for a gerbil but more so for a prize race horse. As an example, a notorious hotelier in New York City left several million dollars for the maintenance of her dog, later reduced by a court to $2m. The dog managed to live to a natural death, despite many threats to end it prematurely.

In Canada, a pet is considered to be property and not a beneficiary; so, leave funds to be administered by your executor or a trusted beneficiary to care for the pet.

1. Will
You could include a provision in your will obligating your executor or a beneficiary to provide an amount of money for the care and maintenance of your pet.[293]

2. Pet Trust
A non-charitable purpose trust for the care and maintenance of a pet.

---

[293] *Pettingall v Pettingall* (1842), 11 LJCh 176.

CHAPTER 17

EDUCATION

Education is no longer just for the young as more adults return to school for continuing education.

1.   Gifting

You can make a gift to a student or to the student's educational institution. An attraction of gifting is that there is no maximum amount to be gifted. A gift usually is a taxable disposition but not for a gift of an asset that is non-appreciating (cash) or appreciating with offsetting losses, exemptions, or tax credits. For a minor, the attribution rules may attribute back to you any income generated by the gift but not capital gains nor secondary income earned on the attributed income.[294]

2.   Student's RESP

You can open a RESP with:

>   1.   you as subscriber,
>
>   2.   (a)   your   spouse/partner   as   joint   subscriber,   or

---

[294]   *ITA* ss 74.1-75.

(b) your executor or a testamentary trust as subsequent subscriber, and

3.   the child or your spouse/partner as beneficiary, whoever will be the student.

If the RESP is set up in this manner, then at your death, your contributions to the RESP do not go into your estate but to your joint or subsequent subscriber.[295] There is a maximum lifetime limit of $50,000 on contributions.

Withdrawals can be the taxable Education Assistance Payment (EAP) or the non-taxable Post-Secondary Education Payment (PSE).

3.   Student's RRSP

If you have a family business, hire and pay your student (child, spouse/partner) an "earned income" who can then open a RRSP, even as a minor with your letter of consent. The student can make contributions, report them on her own tax return, and later make tax-free withdrawals through the Lifelong Learning Plan up to $10,000 per year for a total of $20,000, all to be paid back over 10 years. Earned income for a minor can come also from summer jobs, babysitting, and paper routes.

4.   Informal Trust ("In Trust For" or ITF)

You set up an informal trust at a financial institution "in trust for" your minor child with you as contributor and your spouse/partner as trustee who makes the investment decisions. It is important to have different persons as contributor and trustee to avoid the CRA finding no trust to exist, which could result in income being attributed back to you.

Investments should be growth-oriented to create capital gains rather than income because, for a minor, capital gains are not attributed back to you. There is no maximum limit on contributions. Capital

---

[295]   *ITA* s146.1.

gains should be realized periodically by the child to take advantage of personal tax credits on the child's income tax return. At the age of majority, the child becomes entitled to the trust assets.

5. Life Insurance

One option is to purchase and pay the premiums on a permanent policy on the (grand)child's life at whose majority you transfer the ownership tax-free to the (grand)child who arranges a loan to pay for education.

Another option is to purchase a universal life policy with large funding on the lives of yourself and your (grand)child. When the (grand)child attains the age of majority, you withdraw from the policy and transfer ownership tax-free to the (grand)child who arranges loans to pay for education.[296]

In either case, the loan can be arranged by borrowing from the insurance policy or by using the policy as collateral for a loan from a financial institution.

6. Discretionary Trust

You can arrange a living or testamentary trust with discretion given to the trustee(s) for funding education. There is no maximum amount that can be contributed to the trust. The child's entitlement to the trust assets can be delayed beyond the age of majority, perhaps with an Age 40 Trust. The attribution rules apply to attribute trust income (but not capital gains) back to you while the child is a minor; so, capital should be used to pay for education.

7. Second Career Grants

The Government of Ontario has created a Second Careers program offering grants up to $28,000 for educational costs and living expenses if you are:

---

[296] *ITA* ss148(8)-(8.2).

- laid off or been laid off since January 2005,

- unemployed or working at an interim job, or

- retraining for a career in demand.

The website is "www.secondcareerontario.com".

8. TFSA

A TFSA of you or the student is useful to fund education, especially for an adult who does not qualify for RESP government grants.

CHAPTER 18
REAL ESTATE

18.1 Generally

18.2 Principal residence

18.3 Family home

18.4 Vacation property

18.5 Reverse mortgage

18.6 Life-lease housing

18.1 GENERALLY

As a general rule, you should do a search or at least a sub-search of the title to your real property so that you avoid the problem of dealing with property that you no longer own. Perhaps you've forgotten that transfer you did to your company or to your spouse/partner or children.[297] This is another reason to update your estate documents every few years.

18.2 PRINCIPAL RESIDENCE

In income tax, a disposition of property is considered to be a taxable event. However, there is the concept introduced in 1972 of a "principal residence", which is a "dwelling owned and ordinarily inhabited" by you, your spouse/partner, or child during the year.[298] The inhabitant

---

[297] *Meier v Rose,* 2012 CanLII 82 (ABQB) where a testator forgot that neither he nor his company still owned the land.

[298] *ITA* ss 40(2)(b); 54; ITF S1-F3-C2 *Principal Residence.*

must be a Canadian resident. A principal residence is exempt from income tax and, if passing outside the estate, it also avoids probate.

The property can be a house, apartment, mobile home, trailer, houseboat, vacation property, leasehold interest in a housing unit, or a share of a co-operative housing corporation, located in or outside Canada, plus ½ hectare (1 ¼ acres) of surrounding land.[299]

The CRA has a liberal attitude toward "ordinarily inhabited" which can be a short period of time, such as a vacation.[300]

Until 1982, a family could have two principal residences with each held in sole and not joint ownership.[301] The family can still enjoy the exemption for pre-1982 capital gains on the second dwelling.

A capital loss on a principal residence cannot be claimed because the property is considered in income tax to be "personal use property."

If you have two properties, then claim the exemption on the one with the larger capital gain. The designation can be made annually and can change as a result. Alternatively, consider using a Principal Residence Trust where the property will be used by other family members.

Any disposition of a principal residence must be reported to the CRA (form T2091). A "disposition" can be a sale, death, or divorce. The CRA might deny the exemption if it considers that you are in the business of buying and selling your dwellings.

18.3 FAMILY HOME
The following are the ways of owning and transferring the family home in order to minimize taxation, sometimes using the principal residence exemption.

---

[299] *ITA* s 54 *principal residence.*

[300] *ITF* S1-F3-C2.

[301] *ITA* s 40(4).

1. Spousal Rollover

You can transfer ownership to your spouse/partner on a spousal rollover basis during your lifetime or at your decease. Additionally, the principal residence exemption can be used and continue if both of you have ordinarily inhabited the residence.[302]

2. Joint Tenancy

If the property is ordinarily occupied by both you and your spouse/partner, then placing it in joint tenancy (using the spousal rollover) ensures that a principal residence exemption continues for the survivor. The exemption will similarly continue if a joint interest is created between you and a child who ordinarily resides there.

Be careful if you are an aging parent who wants a married child to move into your home for your care and support. If the child predeceases you, you could end up sharing your home with the child's spouse/partner who decides to sever the joint tenancy thereby creating a tenancy in common to be sold against your wishes. The solution is to have your child:

1. sign a domestic contract with her spouse/partner that, in the event of the child's decease before you, the spouse/partner will not claim an interest in the home, and

2. place a clause in or make a codicil to her will that, in the event of the child's death before you, any interest in the home reverts to you.

3. Remainder Interest to Children

If you wish to allow your spouse/partner to live in the home for life after which it passes to your children, then leave a life interest in the home to your spouse/partner and a remainder interest to your children. This will ensure that your spouse/partner does not sell the home.

---

[302] *ITA* ss 70(6), 73(1).

The creation of two interests results in an immediate taxable disposition of the entire property at fair market value unless the principal residence exemption is used. Income tax on future growth is deferred until final disposition by the last remainder person.[303]

4. Principal residence trust

You use the principal residence exemption to avoid income tax on the transfer and the trustee should make the necessary CRA filings to maintain the exemption. (ITA 107(2), (2.01)). Neither the trust beneficiary nor her spouse can designate another property as principal residence. After 2016, the trust must be alter ego, joint partner, self-benefit, spousal, QDT (qualifying disability), or for a minor of deceased parents.

5. Trust (Personal, Alter Ego, Joint Partner)

Keep in mind that a trust requires setup and maintenance costs. Nevertheless, you can transfer property to one of these trusts by a tax-deferred rollover. If the capital gain is large, then instead use the principal residence exemption so that the trust acquires the property at fair market value in a tax-sheltered way.[304]

If the principal residence exemption is used, then the trust beneficiary should be you, known as the "specified beneficiary" or your spouse/partner, former spouse/partner, or child who ordinarily inhabits the residence. No one else in their family unit should claim the exemption.[305]

18.4 VACATION PROPERTY

A disposition of a vacation property is generally a taxable event for any capital gains realized but there are ways to minimize the tax.

---

[303] *ITA* ss 43.1; IT-226R; *DePedrina v The Queen*, 2005 CanLII 590 (TCC).

[304] *ITA* ss 40(4), 69(1)(b), (c), 73(1), (1.01).

[305] *ITA* s 54 *principal residence* (c1); *ITF* S1-F3-C2.

1. Principal residence exemption

As stated before, the principal residence exemption can apply to a cottage, mobile home, and even a houseboat. The exemption often arises when the owner sells the family home using the principal residence exemption, moves into an apartment, and claims the vacation property as the new principal residence.

At disposal of the vacation property, the income tax due is only on the period when the exemption did not apply before becoming the new principal residence. Pre-1982 capital gains are also excluded if the vacation property was also a principal residence back then.

2. Management Plan & Buy-Sell Agreement

You should create a family management plan of the property that will make everyone aware of their obligations and the consequences of not fulfilling them. Alternatively, you could create a partnership agreement among the children. A fund should be started for repairs and maintenance.

When taking ownership, the children should create a buy-sell agreement (pp. 165-166) with a "shotgun clause" so that one child can name a price for the others to buy him out or to sell to him at that price.

3. Life Insurance

Life insurance on yourself with your estate as beneficiary is a great asset to have available if, after your decease, some family members want the property kept in the family and others want it sold. The latter can be bought out using the insurance proceeds.

4. Joint Tenancy With Right of Survivorship

You create a joint tenancy with your spouse/partner or your children or both. The easiest time to do so is when you purchase the property. A joint tenancy with your spouse/partner can use the spousal rollover.

A joint tenancy with your children will be a taxable event but, additionally, you must be clear in your intention. Two results are possible.

If a gift is intended, then you should execute a deed of gift because, otherwise, the children may be found to be holding the property on a resulting trust for your estate.[306]

5. Gift in Your Will + Life Insurance

You purchase life insurance on yourself with your estate as beneficiary and, in your will, you gift the vacation property to a beneficiary, perhaps a child. At your death, the insurance will offset the estate's probate tax and also income tax on capital gains from the deemed disposition at fair market value. The principal residence exemption can be claimed by the beneficiary if ordinarily residing in the property.

6. Sale to children + Life Insurance

While you are alive or after your death, you arrange for the vacation property to be sold at fair market value to your children thereby transferring future capital gains to them. You or your estate will pay income tax on the capital gains from the sale. If sold by your estate, the tax can be offset by purchasing life insurance on yourself while alive with the estate as beneficiary.

7. Sale + Mortgage /Promissory Note + Life Insurance

While you are alive, you sell the property to your children at fair market value, take back a demand mortgage or promissory note from them with deferred payments over several years, and purchase life insurance on yourself with your estate as beneficiary. The capital gain is taxed over a five-year period. Upon your decease, your estate forgives the mortgage or note, the children are debt-free, and any remaining taxes are offset by the life insurance.

8. Life & Remainder Interests + Life Insurance

When the property is purchased, you create a life interest for yourself and a remainder interest for your children.

---

[306] *Pecore v Pecore,* 2007 CanLII 17 (SCC).

If the interests are created later than at purchase, then you execute a deed of gift to your children and reserve in the deed a life interest to yourself. The creation of two interests results in an immediate taxable disposition of the entire property at fair market value. Income tax on future growth is deferred until final disposition by the last remainder person.[307] Taxes are offset by life insurance on yourself payable to the estate.

9. Testamentary Trust + Life Insurance

Keeping in mind the costs of a trust, you purchase life insurance on yourself with the estate as beneficiary and, in your will, you create a trust to which your executor will transfer the property when you die. At your death, the insurance will offset the estate's probate tax and income tax from the deemed disposition at fair market value. with any excess used to create an endowment for maintenance of the property. The trust can claim the principal residence exemption if a trust beneficiary ordinarily resides in the property.[308]

10. Living Trust

A transfer to a trust is normally a taxable disposition unless the property is the subject of a principal residence exemption. A trust is able to continue the exemption if a trust beneficiary ordinarily resides in the property. If the exemption does not apply, the tax can be deferred using a rollover to a trust that is spousal, alter ego, joint partner, or self-benefit.[309]

11. Purchase as a fractional property

Purchase the property as a "fractional property," which looks like a time-share property but is equity-based rather than use-based, and

---

[307] *ITA* s 43.1; IT-226R archived; *DePedrina v The Queen*, 2005 CanLII 590 (TCC).

[308] *ITA* s 54; ITF S1-F3-C2.

[309] *ITA* s 107(2).

it has far fewer users for a unit, often 10 instead of 52 in a time-share. There are annual fees, an operating budget, and a management team. Your equity interest can be treated like any other real estate. Shares can be distributed to your family.

12. Incorporate

The property can be incorporated with equity shares given to each family member. Income tax on the capital gains would be due on the transfer unless the principal residence exemption applies but the exemption Is lost once the corporation owns the property.

18.5 REVERSE MORTGAGE

A lender loans to you a lump sum of money based on the equity In your home. You retain title until you sell or die or at the end of a "fixed term," at which point, interest, principal, and title are then due. You are responsible for closing costs (appraisal, lawyer, etc.), property taxes, and home repairs.

If the loan has a high adjustable interest rate, it may compound principal and interest to erode quickly your equity. The loan is a first charge registered on the property and secondary financing is usually not permitted. There is no recourse for the lender if you live a long time and the total amount due eventually exceeds the value of the home. If you wish to terminate the reverse mortgage early, you may find it costly with heavy exit penalties.

18.6 LIFE-LEASE HOUSING

A sponsor creates housing units, retains title, and leases units to individuals for their exclusive occupancy and in which they build equity. The equity can be sold at market value with up to 90% of the price retained by the resident and the balance to the sponsor. This is a new concept without much regulatory protection against risks for residents. The sponsor is often a non-profit religious or charitable group. The provinces have information, such as the Ontario Life-Lease Housing Resource Guide.

CHAPTER 19
PROTECTION FROM CLAIMS

Claims can come from many sources:

- creditors of you, of a joint owner, or of a beneficiary, particularly a beneficiary who is a spendthrift or disabled or ill,

- a dependant under dependants' relief legislation,

- a disgruntled family member,

- a spouse under family law, or

- a spouse/partner claiming a valuable asset, like a principal residence, that you really want to go to your children of a prior marriage.

Despite the techniques suggested below, protection from creditors is not always available in the following circumstances:

- a fraudulent conveyance or settlement done to deprive creditors, contrary to provincial law[310] or to federal bankruptcy and criminal law,[311]

- support obligations for a spouse or dependant under provincial law,[312] and

- income taxes owing.[313]

A person with financial problems will usually find it difficult to avoid creditor claims, although death is one proven way to escape creditors if you have no estate left.

The general idea is to use tools so that assets do not go into your estate.

1.   Transfer Wealth to Spouse/Partner

You can use a spousal rollover to transfer capital property on a tax-deferred basis to your spouse/partner without realizing a capital gain or loss until she disposes of the property or dies. The same applies to a spousal trust and to a joint partner trust.[314]

---

[310]   eg. Ontario *Fraudulent Conveyances Act*, RSO 1990, c F.29.

[311]   *An Act to amend the Bankruptcy and Insolvency Act, the Companies' Creditors Arrangement Act, the Wage Earner Protection Program Act and chapter 47 of the Statutes of Canada,* 2005, SC 2007; *Criminal Code*, s 392; *Stone v Stone* (2001), 203 DLR(4th) 257 (OCA); *Abakhan v Braydon*, 2009 CanLII 521 (BCCA).

[312]   *Harrison v State Farm* (1996), 67 ACWS(3d) 1160 (OCGD).

[313]   *ITA* ss 224-225; *MNR v Moss*, 1997 CanLII 5741 (FCTD).

[314]   *ITA* ss 70(6), 73(1); IT-209R, 209RSR.

2. Life insurance

You can shelter from creditors a life insurance policy and payments by naming:[315]

- a successor owner of the policy so that it continues and does not fall into your estate,

- members of a "family class" as beneficiaries:

    - in Quebec: the spouse/partner, ascendants, and descendants of the <u>policyholder</u>, or

    - in the other provinces: the spouse/partner, parent, (grand)child of the <u>life insured</u>,[316] or

- anyone as an irrevocable beneficiary.

There is no protection:

- for you if you are policy owner and beneficiary (or your estate),[317]

- for a beneficiary once he receives payment from a policy, and

- for the side account of a universal life insurance policy.

---

[315] Provincial Insurance Acts:
AB: RSA 2000, c .I-3, s 660;
BC: SBC 2012, c 1, s 59;
MB: CCSM 1987, c.140, s173;
NB: RSNB 1973, c I-12, s157;
NL: RSNL 1990, c L-14, s 27;
NS: RSNS 1989, c 231, s 198;
ON: RSO 1990, c I.8, s196;
QC: *CCQ* art 2457,
SK: SS 1978, c S-26, s 158.

[316] Partner is included in most provinces but not in NB, NL, NU, YT.

[317] For instance, *IA* ss196(1), (2), 171; *CCQ* arts 2456-2460;
Whalley v Harris Steel, 1997 CanLII 1318 (OCA).

3. Annuities

An annuity receives the same protection as life insurance.[318]

4. Segregated funds

The funds receive the same protection as for life insurance outside Quebec.[319] There was some doubt in Quebec but protection has been given if the beneficiary is from the family class or named irrevocably.[320]

5. RPP, IPP

Generally, legislation protects funds within a RPP and IPP from creditor claims[321] but not from claims for dependants' relief [322] nor from income taxes owing.[323] Benefits under the plans that are considered payable or paid can be seized.

6. Discretionary Trust

Transfer property to a trust in which the beneficiaries have no right to claim an interest in the trust.

---

[318] *Tennant v Tennant*, 2002 CanLII 7586 (OCA);
Scotia Capital v Bank of Nova Scotia & Guy Thibault, 2004 CanLII 29 (SCC).

[319] *Re Sykes Bankruptcy*, [1998] 8 WWR 120 (BCCA).

[320] *CCQ* art 2367; *Scotia Capital v Bank of Nova Scotia & Guy Thibault*, op.cit.

[321] Provincial protection exists in BC, AB, SK, MB, ON, PE, NL; eg.
Ontario *Pension Benefits Act*, RSO 1990, c P.8.

[322] eg. Ontario *SLRA*, s 72.

[323] *Sun Life v Canada*, [1992] 4 WWR 504 (SaskQB).
Amherst Crane Rental v Perrin 2004 CanLII 18104 (OCA).

6. RRSP, RRIF

Federally, these plans cannot be seized by creditors[324] and most provinces have amended their laws to provide similar protection. Federal bankruptcy law protects RRSPs and RRIFs for contributions made prior to one year before bankruptcy. Similar results hold true for a spousal RRSP or RRIF, and a LIRA, LIF, and LRIF.

A RRSP or RRIF from a life insurance company is accorded the same protection from creditors as life insurance if the beneficiary is of the family class or designated irrevocably.[325]

7. RESP

A RESP is not a trust and is owned by you, the subscriber, not the beneficiary. At your death, the plan would be part of your estate and subject to probate and creditor claims unless you name your spouse/ partner as joint or subsequent subscriber.

8. Life Insurance Trust

Keep in mind the setup and ongoing maintenance costs of a trust. You purchase a life insurance policy in which you are also the life insured. You create a trust outside your will by a separate trust agreement ("trust deed") or inside your will. You can also insert a clause in the insurance contract referring to the trust in your will. You name beneficiaries of the trust either in the trust deed, in the contract, or in your will. Similar to life insurance, the trust does not form part of your estate because proceeds flow directly to the trust. Multiple insurance trusts for multiple beneficiaries are allowed but, if for one beneficiary, the CRA will group them together.

---

[324] *An Act to amend the Bankruptcy and Insolvency Act, the Compan-ies' Creditors Arrangement Act, the Wage Earner Protection Program Act and chapter 47 of the Statutes of Canada, 2005*, SC 2007, c 36. *Amherst Crane v Perring*, 2004 CanLII 18104 (OCA).

[325] *Royal Bank of Canada v North American Life Insur-ance Co*, 1996 CanLII 219 (SCC).

9.   Discretionary Trusts

You create a discretionary trust so that the income and capital are distributed at the discretion of the trustee and cannot be seized by creditors until paid or payable to a beneficiary. Note that the alter ego, self-benefit, and joint partner trusts do not avoid creditor claims because the beneficiary Is the settlor who creates the trust.

CHAPTER 20
CHARITABLE CONTRIBUTIONS

A "charity" in law is distinguished by providing benefits exclusively for the relief of poverty, advancement of education or religion, or an activity beneficial to a community.[326]

If you expect to receive a charitable tax receipt, check to make sure that the charity is registered with the CRA either by calling or by visiting its website: www.cra-arc.gc.ca/chrts-gvng/menu-eng.html. You will need the exact legal name of the charity.

As you can see from the following list, there are a number of ways in which to benefit a charity.

20.1 Gifting

20.2 Life insurance

20.3 Registered product

20.4 Charitable gift annuity

20.5 Purchase annuity

20.6 Charitable trust

[326] *ITA* ss 149(1)(f), 149.1 *charitable organization*; Tax Guide T4063; *Commissioners for Special Purposes of Income Tax v Pemsel.* [1891] AC 531 (HL).

20.1   GIFTING

Your gift to a charity creates an income tax credit deductible to a maximum of 100% of net income in the year of death or the preceding year and, in the case of a graduated rate estate, the two years preceding the gift.[327] If your estate will have a large taxable income, it may be wise to arrange liquidity (eg. life insurance) so that your executor can make charitable donations to offset the taxable income.

If you do not want to gift all of a particular holding to charity, then gift enough so that the charitable tax receipt offsets the tax due on the sale of the rest of the holding.

If you intend to make a number of charitable donations left to the discretion of your executor, be specific in your charitable intent and in the total dollar amount or percentage.

Cash

This is the usual and easiest method to donate and receive an immediate charitable tax receipt. Donations can be carried forward 5 years. Until 2017 there has been a federal First-Time Donor tax credit to a maximum of $250 (25% on a donation of $1,000) if you have not donated in the prior 5 years.

A donation can be increased by leveraging your non-registered investments using excess cash in the following procedure:

1.   take out a loan and invest the proceeds,

2.   the loan increases your investment portfolio,

---

[327]   *ITA* s118.1; CRA: Estate Donations--Death after 2015.

3. your excess cash pays the interest on the loan,

4. interest payments are tax-deductible, and

5. the resulting tax savings are donated to the charity.

Compounding of the investment also increases the size of donations.

Gift-in-Kind

A gift-in-kind is a tangible asset and not a service. Normally, the giving of a gift-in-kind is a taxable disposition for which you (donor) are required to pay income tax on 50% of the capital gains realized, to be offset by a charitable tax receipt from the charity. A gift Is valued at death for taxes and again at transfer to the charity for the charitable receipt. The tax is avoided by a "zero inclusion rate" on certain property, such as publicly-traded securities (stocks, bonds, funds), certified cultural property, and certified ecological property. You receive a tax receipt for 100% of the value of the gift and avoid paying tax on the gift.[328] The cultural property is certified by the Canadian Cultural Property Export Review Board and the ecological property is certified by Environment Canada.[329] If donating a segregated fund, name the charity as successor owner

If the donated property will cause a large tax liability detrimental to your family, then you should purchase life insurance approximating the value of the property but with an increasing death benefit to cover increases in the value of the property. If you have a spouse/partner, the policy should also be joint last-to-die. Insurance proceeds are received tax-free at your decease.

20.2 LIFE INSURANCE

For a small annual outlay for premiums, life insurance provides a significant gift to a charity, especially because there is no shrinkage

---

[328] *ITA* s 38.

[329] *ITA* ss 118.1(10.1)-(12).

due to taxes, probate, creditor claims, administrative fees and consequent delays. Growth within the policy is tax-free. The insurance may be used in four different ways to benefit both a charity and you.[330]

(1) Assignment of Existing Policy

You assign your existing life insurance policy to the charity with the following result:[331]

1. the charity becomes the owner and makes itself beneficiary of the policy,

2. the assignment is a taxable disposition with your proceeds equal to the <u>cash surrender value</u> of the policy (nil for a term policy) over its cost,

3. you receive a charitable tax receipt for the policy's <u>fair market value</u> (use an actuary to determine), and

4. you receive a tax receipt annually for any premiums that you pay.

(2) Charity is the Beneficiary of Your Policy

You own the policy and designate the charity as beneficiary. The advantages are that you retain control while alive and your estate receives a tax credit when you die, but no credit for premiums paid. The charity receives the proceeds outside the estate and avoids probate.

(3) Donate Through Your Will

A will may be used to gift insurance proceeds to a charity. You own the policy, your estate is the beneficiary, and instructions are left in your will to pay the proceeds to the charity. The advantages are that you retain control over the policy, can change the charity designation

---

[330] *ITA* ss 118.1(1), (5.1), (5.2); IT-244R3; IC-89-3, para's 40, 41.

[331] *ITA* ss 147-148, IC-89-3.

and, at your decease, the charity issues a charitable tax receipt to your estate, thereby offsetting any taxes. The disadvantages are that there is no immediate tax credit for the premiums paid, probate is not avoided, and creditors may make claims against the proceeds in the estate.

(4) Charity Is Policy Owner & Beneficiary

You purchase a new policy on yourself and assign the ownership to the charity that is also the beneficiary or, alternatively, the charity purchases a policy on you. The beneficiary designation need not be irrevocable. You pay the premiums and receive annual tax receipts for the premiums paid. At your death, the charity receives the proceeds outside your estate thereby avoiding probate. The disadvantages are that there is no tax credit to the estate and control is relinquished in favour of the charity.

Split Dollar (or shared ownership) of policy

A variation of charitable ownership of the policy is the split-dollar arrangement of ownership in which you purchase a permanent policy (usually universal life), with the following result:

1. (a) you assign the death benefit part of a new policy on your life to the charity, which names itself as beneficiary of the death benefit (face amount of policy),

    (b) the assignment does not generate a charitable receipt because a new policy has nil value,

    (c) you retain the cash surrender (growth) part of the policy and name a beneficiary for this part,

    (d) you pay the annual premium for both parts and receive a charitable tax receipt for the death benefit premium annually, or

2. (a) you assign the death benefit part to one charity and the cash surrender part to another charity,

(b) each charity names itself beneficiary for its part,

(c) the assignment does not generate a charitable receipt because a new policy has nil value, and

(d) you pay the premiums for each part and receive a charitable tax receipt from each charity annually.

There is a possibility that the assignment of parts of an existing policy would also generate a charitable tax receipt for the value of the part assigned, but this may be difficult to calculate.

20.3   REGISTERED PRODUCT
Similar to life insurance, a donation can also be made by designating, where possible, a charity as beneficiary in a registered product (eg. RRSP).[332] The proceeds are included in your estate's income and then given to the charity which issues a charitable tax receipt for the same amount to offset up to 100% of income tax.

20.4   CHARITABLE GIFT ANNUITY
This involves work for the charity and is used by larger charities (eg. hospital foundation, university). You are probably an older retired client looking for guaranteed income for life.

You make a lump-sum donation irrevocably to a charity on the understanding that the charity will provide you with a stream of guaranteed income for a fixed period of time or for life. The annuity can be made joint-and-survivor to provide income eventually for your surviving spouse/partner when you die.

You receive an immediate tax receipt for the lump sum less the fair market cost of the annuity. The charity has the use of the difference between the lump sum and the annuity cost. The annuity payments to you are comprised of taxable interest and non-taxable return of

[332]   *ITA* ss 118.1(5.1)-(5.3); IT-297R2.

capital. The money donated to the charity can be replaced by purchasing life insurance on yourself with your estate as beneficiary.

20.5 PURCHASE ANNUITY

Often used for smaller charities, you simply purchase an annuity for a guaranteed income and donate an excess amount to the charity for an immediate tax receipt. Again, the annuity can be made joint-and-survivor to provide income for your surviving spouse/partner when you die. The money donated can be replaced by purchasing life insurance on yourself with your estate as beneficiary.

The tax receipt to you is the same as in **20.4.** For example, in **20.4,** you donate say $100,000 to a charity which purchases an annuity for $50,000 and issues to you a tax receipt for the excess $50,000. In **20.5**, you purchase the annuity for $50,000 and donate to the charity $50,000 which issues to you a tax receipt. The latter is less work for the charity.

A variant of you purchasing the annuity is to have the charity act as your agent in purchasing the annuity so that the charity has more control to ensure that you will make the donation to it.

20.6 CHARITABLE TRUST

A living or testamentary trust with charitable purposes and an exemption from taxation if a registered charity.[333]

20.7 CHARITABLE REMAINDER TRUST

For a lifetime of income and then a donation to a charity, you create a charitable remainder trust with the charity named as the irrevocable capital beneficiary. For a living trust, you retain a lifetime possession of the property and receive any trust income until death and then the asset as capital is gifted to the charity. For a testamentary trust, the lifetime income is paid to a trust beneficiary at whose death the property is gifted to the charity.

---

[333] *ITA* ss 149(1)(f), 149.1 *charitable organization*; Tax Guide T4063.

The tax situation is more complex. The transfer of property to the trust is a taxable disposition because the donation is not directly to the charity. You can elect proceeds of disposition between the fair market value and cost base of the property, and the elected amount is used to calculate the value of the remainder interest for the tax receipt from the charity.[334]

The spousal, alter ego and joint partner trusts, are ideal vehicles because the assets are rolled to the trust on a tax-deferred basis with income going to you or your partner for life with no encroachment on capital.[335] Probate and challenges to the trust are avoided.

20.8 NON-CHARITABLE PURPOSE TRUST

The objects of this trust are not exclusively charitable but can be a combination of charitable and non-charitable, such as to maintain graves or pets. Tax results are similar to the above trusts.

20.9 PRIVATE FOUNDATION

A private foundation is a registered charity owned by a donor[336] who receives various benefits:

- targeted philanthropy,

- public recognition,

- control of investments, donations, and recipients,

- privacy, especially necessary if the investments are your private company shares, and

- co-ordination with estate and tax planning.

---

[334] *ITA* s 118.1(6); *Charitable Remainder Trust*, CSP-C02; IT-226R archived, paras 5-8.

[335] IT-226R archived.

[336] *ITA* ss 149.1(1) *charitable foundation*, 149.2, 188.1.

However, there are costly drawbacks that limit them to the wealthy:

- regulatory oversight,[337]

- professional costs of setup and ongoing maintenance (lawyers, accountants),

- inability to carry on commercial activity, and

- CRA's various reporting requirements.

20.10 DONOR-ADVISED FUNDS

Public foundations and financial institutions have created donor-advised funds to serve multiple clients who want the private foundation experience of the wealthy without setup costs and administrative responsibilities. You have a separate account in your name (eg. "The Jones Endowment for the Environment") and have control over choosing the charity and your investments. Annually the foundation advises you of the amount available to grant to charities and makes the donation for you. A minimum initial investment, usually $10,000 to $50,000 is required, which can be cash, life insurance, or publicly-traded stocks, bonds, or funds. The foundation is registered with the CRA as a charitable, non-profit organization so that it can issue tax receipts for donations.

[337] *David Feldman Charitable Foundation,* 1987 CanLII 4364 (OSC).

CHAPTER 21
BUSINESS TRANSITION

21.1 GENERALLY

A business creates a special case in estate planning for which there are various considerations:

- to continue the business or to dispose of it,

- succession planning to the family or to others (eg. employees),

- support for yourself and dependants via the business,

- will and trust planning for property transference,

- retention of control, and

- minimization or deferral of taxes.

"Corporate attribution rules" are designed to catch income and capital gains when there is a transfer or loan to a corporation for the purpose of reducing the transferor's income and providing a benefit to a spouse/partner, spousal trust, minor (grand)child, or a niece or nephew, in which case you are deemed to receive the income.[338] The rules do not apply if the recipient corporation is a "small business corporation" or the above individuals own less than 10% of the corporation, or you are non-resident.

21.2   GIFT OR SALE OF THE BUSINESS

If you gift your business or sell it for less than fair market value, the transfer will be deemed to have occurred at fair market value for income tax purposes.[339] Income tax can be deferred for a private corporation where the transfer is rolled at your cost to your spouse or to a trust that is spousal, alter ego, joint partner, or self-benefit.[340] Capital gains can be sheltered if any of the exemptions apply (small business, farming, fishing). If a family business, insert a clause that, in the event of a marital breakdown, the disposition Is not part of "net family property."

21.3   LIFE INSURANCE

For protection from creditors, the beneficiary of insurance owned by a corporation should be named irrevocably.

1.   Key Person Insurance

Key Person Insurance is owned by the corporation on valuable personnel like yourself. Assuming you are the owner of the business, the insurance provides the funds to purchase your business interest directly from your estate or to create a fund for your living buyout or your retirement.

---

[338]   *ITA* ss 74.1-74.4.

[339]   *ITA* s 69(1).

[340]   *ITA* s 73(1).

CANADIAN ESTATE PLANNING MADE EASY

2. Buy-Sell Agreement

A buy-sell agreement among shareholders of a corporation contains the conditions for transfer of share ownership upon certain events, such as death, disability, retirement, bankruptcy, or marital break-down. It creates a market for the shares with a price determined ahead or by formula. An agreement assures employees and creditors of a continuation of the business and helps your executor to pay estate taxes. Universal life insurance is often used as a tax-free funding mechanism. A spousal rollover is not available. Any capital gain is taxable to the deceased's estate but may be sheltered by an exemption. Typical agreements follow:

In a **Cross-Purchase ("Criss-cross") Agreement**, each owner buys insurance on the other owners and makes himself beneficiary. The survivors use the proceeds to buy the deceased's portion of the business thereby creating an increased cost base for that portion. The deceased's estate bears any tax on capital gains.

In a **Promissory Note Buy-Sell Agreement**, the corporation owns and is beneficiary of insurance on the shareholders. When one of them dies, the survivors buy out the deceased's estate with a promissory note covered by the corporation paying the insurance proceeds to the survivors. The estate bears the tax on any capital gain and the survivors receive the deceased's portion of the business with an increased cost base. A variation is a **Hybrid Buy-Sell Agreement** in which a variable number of shares may be bought if the estate is in a position to shelter the capital gains on them.

In a **Corporate Share Redemption**, there is an obligation on each shareholder's estate to sell and on the corporation to redeem the deceased's shares. The corporation owns life insurance on the shareholders and is also beneficiary. The corporation uses the insurance proceeds to purchase the deceased's shares.

Another Buy-Sell variation is the **Split Dollar** (or shared ownership) of the permanent life insurance jointly owned by the business and an executive person. A formal legal agreement is made with the following procedure:

1. the business owns the death benefit,

2. the executive Is the life insured and owner of the cash surrender value of the policy,

3. each owner pays a relevant portion of the premium, and

4. at retirement the business assigns the death benefit portion to the executive (probably no taxable policy gain).

The business has coverage in the event of death and the executive has tax-deferred growth and eventually ownership of the entire policy.

21.4 SMALL BUSINESS

A capital gains exemption of $835,716 is available when you dispose of shares of your "qualified" small business. The shares must be owned by you, your spouse/partner, or a partnership related to you.[341] If the business is to be transferred into a trust, remember that only a spousal trust has access to the exemption.[342]

The corporate attribution rules do not apply to a loan or transfer to a "small business corporation." To avoid monitoring the "small business" status, a family trust can be used to hold the shares.

21.5 FARMING OR FISHING

You can transfer your farming or fishing business in a tax-advantaged manner by using a rollover or a tax exemption.

Rollover

You can defer income tax on capital gains, recaptured depreciation, and land when you transfer them to your child who used the property in the business, which he intends to carry on. The transfer occurs at

---

[341] *ITA* ss 110.6(1), (2.1).

[342] *ITA* s 110.6(12).

a price chosen between the cost of the business and its fair market value.[343]

Qualified Farming of Fishing Exemption

Similar to a qualified small business, an indexed capital gains exemption of $1 million exists for a "qualified" farming or fishing business.[344] The property can be transferred back to you.[345] Determination of "qualification" is complicated and requires con-sultation with an income tax professional. The federal 2015 budget effectively raised the exemption to $1m.

If the farming or fishing business is to be transferred into a trust, remember that only a spousal trust has access to the exemption, especially after your death.[346]

21.6 SPOUSAL ROLLOVER

You can transfer capital property to your spouse/partner so that the recognition of taxable gains is deferred until disposition either by the spouse or when the spouse dies.[347]

If your estate has capital losses or there exists a capital gains exemp-tion, then it may be more advantageous not to use the rollover but to dispose of capital property at fair market value, thereby realizing any taxable capital gains to be offset by the losses or exemption. The choice of whether to use a rollover or realize a gain can be made on a property-by-property basis.

---

[343]   *ITA* ss 70(9), 73(3), (4); IT-349R3 archived.

[344]   *ITA* ss 110.6(1), (2), (2.2).

[345]   *ITA* ss 70(9)-(10); 73(1)-(4); IT-349R3.

[346]   *ITA* s 110.6(12).

[347]   *ITA* s 70(6); IT-305R4.

21.7 TRUSTS

A trust is useful to ensure continuity of your business, especially if your family is involved in it, but it does have setup and maintenance costs that probably can be arranged as tax-deductible.

Family Trust

A family trust is useful in a business context:

- to judge over time the competence of the next generation to run the business,

- to split business income with the next generation, and

- to avoid creditors.

The family trust acquires shares in your family business at fair market value, which may result in a taxable capital gain.

Spousal Trust

A spousal trust is used to provide a lifetime income to the spouse without involving the spouse in the business while the trustees are the rest of the family. The trust is set up to receive shares of a family business at cost on a tax-deferred rollover basis. As stated previously, a spousal trust is the only trust that can claim the capital gains exemptions for a qualified small business, farming, or fishing.[348]

21.8 ESTATE FREEZES

Assuming that you own a business, an estate freeze is a useful tool for two reasons. Firstly, it is used to fix or "freeze" ahead of your death the maximum income tax on capital gains based on your ownership of the business. Secondly, it can pass future growth of the business to the next generation.

For instance, assume your business will continue to grow and, as a consequence, the capital gain on the business also grows. If you

---

[348] *ITA* s 110.6(12).

continue the business until death, the income tax on capital gains will be larger than if you had transferred the business to your children well ahead of death so that they have the growth in capital gains rather than yourself. Freezing the fair market value of your business now and passing the future growth of the business to the next generation will decrease the income tax on the capital gains owed by you. Obviously, a freeze only makes sense if the business is expected to appreciate over time.

Typically, a freeze involves:

- an owner, known as the "freezor" who can be a resident or non-resident, a trust, partnership, or corporation,[349] and

- a corporation having two classes of shares: shares without growth ("freeze shares") and shares with growth ("growth shares").

The freeze shares receive the current value of the corporation while the growth shares are issued at nominal value to others or to a family trust. Freeze shares are redeemable at their freeze-time value, pay dividends, and have a preference on liquidation.

A "wasting estate freeze" occurs when you redeem the freeze shares over time in order to reduce the taxes at your death. Your ultimate tax bill is not only frozen but also reduced.

The advantages of a freeze are:

- possible retention of control by you (the "freezor"),

- a stream of retirement income created as you redeem freeze shares over time,

- passing growth to the next generation,

- reducing taxes,

[349]   *ITA* s 85(1).

- income–splitting by sending income to family members in lower tax brackets, and

- possible multiple uses of capital gains exemptions when family members sell their parts of the business in the future.

Types of Freezes

1. Sale or Gift of Growth Shares

The easiest freeze is a simple sale or gift of your growth shares in your business corporation:

- to the next generation,

- to a new corporation owned by the next generation,

- to a family trust, or

- back to the corporation which then issues the growth shares to the next generation.

If you wish to retain some control over the business, then you can:

- make the freeze shares also the voting shares,

- receive payment from the buyers by a demand note that can be called at any time, or

- make the sale/gift to a discretionary trust or holding corpo- ration to hold the growth shares but otherwise be controlled by you.

From an income tax perspective, the tax liability is immediate on capital gains realized on a sale or gift,[350] which may not be a problem if you wish to offset any gain with capital losses, exemptions, or tax credits. Attribution rules may apply.

---

[350]   *ITA* s 69(1)(b).

2. Income Tax Deferred Freezes

(1) Section 85 Asset Exchange[351]

The steps involved are:

1. you have an existing business with assets (Opco),

2. you create a new taxable Canadian corporation as a holding company (Holdco) that has common and preferred shares,

3. (a) you sell Opco assets to Holdco in exchange for Holdco preferred shares at an elected proceeds of disposition (and possibly a promissory note),

   (b) the sale may trigger a capital gain on the assets unless the elected proceeds are at cost; any gain may be sheltered from income tax by an exemption or capital loss,

   (c) the sale crystallizes the current value of Opco.

4. your children purchase Holdco common shares for nominal value, and receive the future growth of Opco.

Holdco may allow you to retain some control of the business, protection from creditors, and to realize income as you call in the promissory note.

A variation is the **Drop Down Freeze** in which a new corporation is created by the next generation. You transfer the existing corporation's assets to the new corporation in exchange for fixed value preferred shares of the new corporation with a redemption amount equal to the value of assets transferred.

---

[351] *ITA* s 85; IC76-19R3, IT-291R3.

(2) Section 86 Share Exchange[352] (Internal Freeze)

No new corporation is formed. An existing corporation is reorganized in which all of your common shares are exchanged for fixed value preferred shares with a fair market value equal to the value of the corporation. The common shares are now sold to your children at nominal value and they receive the future growth of the corporation. The capital gains exemptions cannot be used because there is no gain nor loss.

(3) Section 51 Share/Debt Exchange[353]

You exchange some or all of your shares for other shares or convertible debt in the corporation. The exchange does not involve a taxable disposition. Any capital gain is deferred until there is disposal of the other shares or debt. No loss can be recognized. Non-share consideration is not allowed.

(4) Stock Dividend Freeze

No new corporation is created. The existing corporation declares a stock dividend to you of new fixed value preferred shares ("stock dividend shares") with a redemption amount equal to the value of the corporation, which is frozen in the preferred shares. New common shares are purchased by the next generation at nominal value. The income tax attribution rules are avoided because there has been no transfer of property.[354]

(5) Section 87 Amalgamation of Corporations

A new corporation is created by amalgamating two or more related corporations that are to be frozen. The new corporation issues freeze shares to you and growth shares to the next generation. The

---

[352] *ITA* s 86.

[353] *ITA* s 51(1).

[354] *ITA* s 74.4(2).

freeze shares embody the frozen value of the new corporation and the growth shares have nominal value. Non-share consideration is not allowed.

(6) Net Family Property Freeze

This freeze is designed to circumvent the family law regarding an equalization payment of net family property on the breakdown of marriage of a member of the next generation. The freezor does an ordinary freeze but gifts the new common/growth shares to the next generation rather then having them purchase the shares. As gifts, the shares are excluded from the calculation of "net family property" if the marriage of the next generation breaks down.[355]

An estate freeze is a complex area and, in addition to income tax implications and traps, consideration must also be given to other federal and provincial legislation in areas, such as shareholder rights, sales taxes, bulk-sales legislation, creditor consents, fraudulent conveyances, family law, among others. It is advisable to seek the services of a professional familiar with the area of estate freezes.

---

[355] *McNamee v McNamee,* 2010 CanLII 533 (ONCA).
Reisman v Reisman, 2014 CanLII 109 (ONCA).

CHAPTER 22
CONFIDENTIALITY

Anything passing outside your estate and/or avoiding publicly-available probate documents will automatically provide a measure of confidentiality, such as the following techniques:.

1. **Life Insurance**

2. **Segregated Funds**

3. **Trusts**

    Some trusts do not form part of the estate:

    - Alter Ego Trust

    - Joint Partner Trust

    - Self-Benefit Trust

    - Qualified Disposition Trust

    - Life Insurance Trust

    - RRSP/RRIF Trust

    - Secret Trust.

4. **Multiple Wills**

In one will are assets not requiring probate (eg. personal effects) and in another will are assets necessitating probate (eg. large bank accounts). The former assets are of a type not requiring court authority to be valid.

APPENDIX A
ESTATE QUESTIONNAIRE

YOUR PARTICULARS

Full Legal Name & Titles:

_____

SIN #:_____

Date & Place of Birth:_____

Citizenship:_____

Citizenship Card/Passport #:_____

Country of Residence:_____

Armed forces veteran? Yes ( ) No ( )

Rank & Serial #: _____

Veterans Card: Yes ( ) No ( ) Discharge papers?

Receiving veterans' benefits: Yes ( ) No ( )

ADDRESSES

Home: _____

Telephone:_____

Email:_____

Business:_____

Telephone:_____

Email:_____

Vacation:_____

HEALTH

Health card #:_____

Organ Donation: Yes ( ) No ( )

Where located (will, donor card, driver's licence):_____

Health records: copies

EMPLOYMENT

Occupation & Employer:

_____

_____

Previous & Employers:

_____

_____

ORGANIZATIONS

Schools, Colleges, Universities & Degrees:

_____

_____

Fraternities:

_____

_____

Activities:

Service Clubs, Positions, Awards:

_____

_____

_____

Public Office & Positions:

_____

_____

CONTACTS (NAME, PHONE, EMAIL)

Executor/Estate Trustee:

_____

_____

Lawyer:

_____

_____

Accountant:

_____

_____

Health Professional:

_____

_____

Preferred Hospital:

_____

_____

Financial Advisor:

_____

_____

Insurance Group & Member #:

_____

_____

Insurance Agent (Life):

_____

_____

Insurance Agent (house, car):

_____

_____

Tax Preparer:

_____

_____

Trustee(s):

_____

_____

Religious Leader:

_____

_____

Trust officer:

_____

_____

Employer/Business partners:

_____

_____

Condominium Corp.:

_____

_____

Landlord:

_____

_____

PARENTS, SIBLINGS, DESCENDANTS

**For children, note if adopted, disabled, married &
spouse, their children, children of prior marriages.**

Name, address, birth date, relationship:

_____

_____

_____

_____

_____

_____

_____

_____

_____

_____

_____

_____

_____

_____

_____

PETS: How will they be cared for:

_____

_____

_____

MARITAL STATUS

Single ( ) Married ( )   Partner ( ) Separated ( )

Divorced ( ) Widow(er) ( )

SPOUSE/PARTNER:

Name:

_____

SIN #:

_____

Date & Place of Birth:_____

Address:_____

Telephone:(Home)

_____

(Business)_____

Email:_____

Date & Place of Marriage:_____

Marriage Licence: Yes( ) No ( ) Copy?

Domestic Contract/Pre-Nuptial Agreement:

Yes ( ) No ( ) Copy? Date, Place, Parties to contract: _____

**Are you to leave some/all of your assets
to your spouse or children?**

At your death, how is your spouse to be provided for?

1. Outright bequest ( ) or lump sum ( )?

**2. Spousal Trust: for spouse's life and then
to children at death of dependant**

Paying income out of trust?

Yes ( ) No ( )

Paying capital out of trust?

Yes ( ) No ( )

When should trust be finally distributed? On death of spouse?

_____

3. Insurance proceeds:

4. Separate Property:

Separation/Divorce/Annulment/Decease
Date & Place:_____

Decrees:_____

Continuing obligations:_____
Until:_____

Will spouse have interest in your estate by means of separation   agreement as a dependant or terms of agreement?:

Yes ( ) No ( ) Copy?

INCOME

	$Monthly	$Annually
Employment Salary		
Bonuses		
Net Income from following:		
Professional		
Business		
Commissions		
Partnerships		
Rent		
Investment Income:		
Dividends		
Interest		
Annuities, RRSP, RRIF		
Pension Income:		
Canada Pension Plan		
Old Age Security		
Other Income:		
Family Allowance		
Disability Payments		
Support Payments		
Alimony		
Other income		
TOTAL ANNUAL INCOME		

BANK ACCOUNTS, GICS AND OTHER DEPOSITS

BRANCH & ADDRESS	ACCT HOLDER	ACCT TYPE, #	BALANCE

CREDIT CARDS & CHARGE ACCOUNTS

COMPANY	ACCT HOLDER	ACCT TYPE, #, PIN	BALANCE

INVESTMENT ASSETS (ATTACH LAST STATEMENTS)

Type (stocks, bonds, funds), approximate value, location, beneficiaries for registered assets.

Flow-through Interests, Limited Partnerships, Trusts:

Tax Shelters:

INSURANCE

POLICIES OWNED BY YOU ON YOUR LIFE

Name of Company:_____

Name of Owner:_____

Insured/Joint Insureds:_____

Premium and Frequency: _____Policy No.: _____

Death benefit & riders:_____
Cash Surrender Value: _____Loans: _____

Named Beneficiaries (irrevocable?): _____
_____

Type of Insurance, Term, Permanent, Group/Other: _____

Insurance Advisor/Broker: _____

POLICIES THAT YOU OWN ON OTHERS

Name of Company:_____

Name of Owner:_____

Insured/Joint Insureds:_____

Premium and Frequency: _____Policy No.:_____

Death benefit & riders: _____

Cash Surrender Value:_____Loans:_____

Named Beneficiaries (irrevocable?): _____
_____

Type of Insurance, Term, Permanent, Group/Other: _____

Insurance Advisor/Broker:_____

POLICIES THAT OTHERS OWN ON YOUR LIFE

Name of Company:_____

Name of Owner:_____

Insured/Joint Insureds: _____

Premium and Frequency: _____Policy No.:_____

Death benefit & riders: _____

Cash Surrender Value: _____Loans: _____

Named Beneficiaries (irrevocable?): _____
_____

Type of Insurance, Term, Permanent, Group/Other:_____

Insurance Advisor/Broker: _____

ANNUITIES

Name of Company:_____

Name of Owner:_____

Payments & Frequency: _____

Annuity No.:_____

Cash Surrender Value: _____
_____

Named Beneficiaries (irrevocable?): _____
_____

Insurance Advisor/Broker:_____

DEATH BENEFITS

From your company: _____

From government (eg Veterans Affairs):_____

From others: _____

REAL ESTATE ASSETS

(a) Type: i.e. residential, commercial, farm, condominium, time-share:

_____

Principal residence for income tax purposes?: Yes ( ) No ( )

Do you consider this to be your matrimonial home? Yes ( ) No ( )

(b) Street Address:

_____

(c) Fair Market Value, Assessed Value, Acquisition Cost & Date, Tax Receipts:

_____

(d) Title registered in the name of:

_____

Joint Tenancy or Tenancy in Common (each has separate interest):

_____

(e) Encumbrances:

_____

(f) Mortgages: (list mortgagee, term, amount, interest, rate):_____

Equity of mortgagor:_____

Reverse Mortgage?_____

(g) Rented: Written copy, Term, Tenant's name/address:

_____

(h) Agreements for Purchase & Sale:

_____

(i) Property insurance certificates: _____

(j) Keys:_____

(k) Maintenance contracts, bills:_____

(l) Tax records:_____

Notes:

BUSINESS INTERESTS

NAME:_____

YOUR POSITION:_____

TYPE: proprietor ( ) partnership ( ) corporation ( )

incorporation date:_____

federal ( ) provincial ( ) where:_____

PROPORTION of ownership (%):_____

TYPE (units, shares):_____

NATURE OF BUSINESS: _____

ADDRESS: _____

CONTACT (tel./email): _____

FAIR MARKET VALUE:

of business: $_____

of your interest: $_____

SHARE STRUCTURE:

# of classes of shares: _____

# of each class of share:_____

classes that have voting rights: _____

YOUR SHARES:

_____

estimated Adjusted Cost Base (ACB): _____

estimated Current Value: _____

paid-up capital of each class (generally an amount returnable tax free):_____

dividend amounts paid annually:_____

on disposition of the shares, do you intend to claim the $800,000 capital gains exemption? Yes ( ) No ( )

BUSINESS LOANS:

Do you have any business loans? Yes ( ) No ( )

Is this a reduced interest loan? Yes ( ) No ( )

Have you personally guaranteed any business loans? Yes ( ) No ( )

RESTRICTIONS ON TRANSFERS OF INTEREST:

_____

SHAREHOLDERS' or BUY/SELL AGREEMENT: copy?

_____

Will your death force an offer to sell?

Yes( ) No ( )

Agreed price under agreement:_____

Will the price bind your estate? Yes ( ) No ( )

LIFE INSURANCE ARRANGEMENTS:

among shareholders or partners to fund a transfer of interest? Yes ( ) No ( )

State amount:_____

CONTINUATION OF BUSINESS: by whom?

_____

Will your spouse or children have an interest? Yes ( ) No ( )

Describe interest: _____

COMPANY BENEFITS:

Insurance:

Group life_____

Corporated-owned_____

Disability_____

Pension:_____

Deferred profit-sharing plan:_____

Retiring allowance:_____

OTHER MAJOR OWNERS (WITH %):

_____

_____

ASSETS & VALUES:

Fixed assets value:_____

Inventory value:_____

Intangibles (copyright, patent, royalty):_____

_____

Copies of latest financial statements.

OTHER ASSETS

[Provide Description, Approx. Value, Ownership, Keys]

(1)   Automobiles, Boats, Recreation Vehicles (include registrations, insurance, lease)

_____

_____

_____

(2)   Farm Machinery, Tools, Livestock, Quotas:

_____

_____

_____

(3)   Heirlooms, Artwork, Jewellry, Collections:

_____

_____

_____

(4)   Household Goods of Value, Furniture, Large Purchases (include warranties):

_____

_____

_____

(5)   Firearms (licences, permits, keys to locker):

_____

(6)   Affinity/Loyalty Programs, card #'s:

_____

_____

_____

(7)   Safety Deposit Boxes

[where, box #, name registered, key location]:

_____

(8)   Are you a beneficiary of any estate or trust?

Are you receiving benefits under an estate?

State name of estate/trust, who administers, amount to which you are entitled

_____

_____

_____

(9)   Have you set up a trust to benefit another person? If so, please give particulars.

_____

_____

_____

(10)   Are there any promissory notes owing you?:

[who owes. amount, due date]

_____

(11)   Technological assets, passwords, websites:

_____

_____

_____

(12)   Do you exercise any powers of appointment over assets of another?: Yes ( ) No ( )

_____

Are you a trustee for someone else or do you
hold assets in your name for someone?

[for whom, amount]

_____

DEBTS, OBLIGATIONS, TAXES:

(1)   Support payments to dependants, spouse?

[Name, amount, frequency, term, arrears]

_____

_____

_____

(2)   Credit Cards:

_____

_____

_____

(3)   Personal or Business Loans, Lines of Credit Owing, Charitable Pledges:

_____

_____

_____

4)   Guarantees given? [To whom, liability]:

_____

(5)   Are you an Executor of an estate or custodian of property? Particulars:

_____

_____

_____

(6) **Legal actions pending by or against you? [Court, claim, estimated liability]:**

_____

_____

_____

(7) **Mortgages payable by you:**

[amount owing, mortgagee, and maturity]

_____

_____

_____

(8) **Taxes Owing:** _____

Copies of tax returns for last 7 years

Notes

YOUR WILL & POWERS OF ATTORNEY:

Location or a copy:_____

Date:_____

Codicils to the will? Location:_____

Witnesses (name, address):_____

_____

_____

Affidavit of execution? Yes ( ) No ( )

Executors and Contingent Executors (if an Executor does not act) to administer your estate:

[Name, address, occupation, relationship]

_____

_____

_____

ATTORNEYS FOR MANAGEMENT OF PROPERTY & FOR HEALTHCARE:
[Name, address, occupation, relationship]

_____
_____
_____

FUNERAL ARRANGEMENTS

Religion:_____

Service: Religious, Veterans, K of C?_____

Eulogy: achievements, happy times, words of wisdom

Favourite readings, hymns:_____
_____

Have you already made arrangements: Yes ( ) No ( )

Which funeral home:_____

Address & Phone:_____

Cremation?: Yes ( ) No ( )

Where?_____

Burial Plot?: Yes ( ) No ( )

Where?_____

Monument/Mausoleum arranged: Yes ( ) No ( )

If you have no funeral arrangements, how will your funeral be paid?
_____

Have you drafted an obituary? Yes ( ) No ( )

With a favourite photo?

Which newspaper(s)?_____
_____
_____

Online? Website?_____

THINGS TO BE CANCELLED

Pre-authorised payments or automatic withdrawals from your bank:

Subscriptions:

_____

_____

_____

Memberships/Clubs:

_____

_____

_____

PropertyInsurance:

_____

_____

_____

Appointments:_____

Rent:_____

Automatic debits: _____

_____

_____

Cable/Internet Provider:_____

_____

_____

Executor of another's estate:_____

APPENDIX B
ACRONYMS

REGULATORS

IIROC—Investment Industry Regulatory Organization of Canada

SC—Securities Commission (provincial govt)

   eg. OSC is Ontario Securities Commission

FSC—Financial Services Commission

   regulates insurance (provincial govt)

   eg. FSCO is Financial Services Commission of Ontario,

   others have Superintendent of Insurance

OSFI   Office of Superintendent of Financial Institutions (federal)

FINANCIAL INDUSTRY

AIFA   Accredited Investment Industry Analyst

AIFP   Accredited Investment Fiduciary Professional

CA   Chartered Accountant

CBV   Chartered Business Valuator

CDFA   Certified Divorce Financial Analyst

CEA   Certified Executor Advisor

CFA   Chartered Financial Analyst

CFP®   Certified Financial Planner®

CGA   Certified General Accountant

CH.F.C.®   Chartered Financial Consultant®

CHS™   Certified Health Insurance Specialist™

CIFP   Registered Financial & Retirement Advisor

CIM®   Chartered Investment Manager®

CIWM   Certified International Wealth Manager

CLU®   Chartered Life Underwriter®

CMA   Certified Management Accountant

CPA   Certified Public Accountant

CPCA   Certified Professional Consultant on Aging (formerly CSA)

CRC   Certified Retirement Counselor

CSA   Certified Senior Advisor

DMS   Derivatives Market Specialist

EPC   Elder Planning Counselor

F.Pl.   Financial Planner (Quebec)

FCSI®   Fellow of Canadian Securities Institute®

FDS   Financial Divorce Specialist

FMA   Financial Management Advisor

FRM   Financial Risk Manager

MTI®   MTI Estate and Trust Professional®

PFP®   Personal Financial Planner®

PRM   Professional Risk Manager

R.F.P.®   Registered Financial Planner®

RHU®   Registered Health Underwriter®

RIAC   Responsible Investment Advisor Certification

RIPC   Responsible Investment Professional Certification

LEGAL INDUSTRY

J.D.   Juris Doctor (U.S. 1st degree in law)

LL.B.   Bachelor of Laws (Canadian 1st degree)

LL.L.   Licence en droit civil (Quebec 1st degree)

LL.M.   Master of Laws (2nd degree)

S.J.D.   Doctor of Juridical Science (3rd degree).

APPENDIX C

DOCUMENTATION TO BRING TO INTERVIEW

1. Recent Income Tax CRA Notice of Assessment

2. Employer and group benefits, and pension plan.

3. Business financial statements, CRA Notice of Assessment.

4. Business partnership and/or shareholder and/or buy-sell agreement(s).

5. Insurance policies: Life, Disability, Critical Illness, Long Term care

6. Latest notices showing status, loans, premiums, dividends, and income replacement amounts

7. Investment statements, including RRSPs, RRIFs, TFSAs, etc.

8. Current debts: mortgages, loans, lines of credit, credit cards, support payments.

9. Will and Powers of Attorney.

10. Domestic Agreements: pre-nuptial, marital, separation, divorce, cohabitation.

11. Trust documents if you or family members are beneficiaries.

INDEX

CPSIA information can be obtained
at www.ICGtesting.com
Printed in the USA
LVOW11s2152270318
571335LV00002B/194/P